Canoeing the

Boundary Waters

The Account of One Family's Explorations

by Marion Stresau

Signpost Books

OTHER SIGNPOST BOOKS FOR THE OUTDOORS

Backpacking With Babies and Small Children
Packrat Papers #1 (Equipment, etc.)
Packrat Papers #2 (Food, etc.)
The Bicycle: A Commuting Alternative
Mostly In Fun
Pacific Crest Trail Hike Planning Guide
Understanding Avalanches
Volunteer Vacations on America's Public Lands
Trails of the Sawtooth and White Clouds (Idaho)
177 Free Oregon Campgrounds
Kayak and Canoe Trips in Washington (Revised)
Snow Tours in Washington (Revised)
Rock Climbing Guide—Leavenworth and Index (Washington)
Whatcom County (Washington) Bike Book
Winter Walks and Summer Strolls—I (near Bellingham)
Hiking the Inland Empire (Spokane)

Write for free descriptive brochure

Signpost Books welcomes inquiries from authors
about prospective books. Suggestions for new
titles also are welcome.

SIGNPOST BOOKS
8912 192nd SW
Edmonds, WA   98020

Edited by Betty Mueller

Cover design by Sue Kemp

Contents

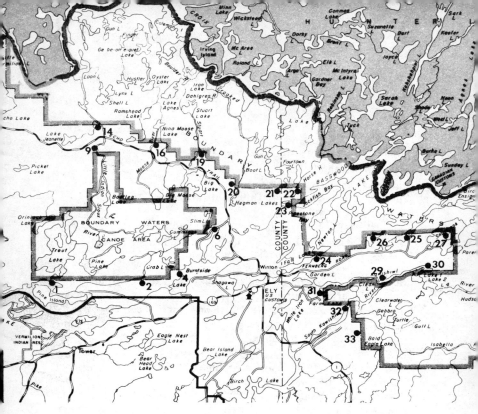

BWCA ENTRANCE POINTS
(Numbered West to East)

1. Trout Lake (from Vermilion)

2. Phantom Lake

4. Crab Lake (from Burntside)

6. Slim Lake

9. Little Indian Sioux River (south of Echo Trail)

12. Little Vermilion Lake (Crane Lake)

14. Little Indian Sioux River (North of Echo Trail)

16. Moose River

19. Stuart River

20. Angleworm Trail 159

21. Fourtown Lake

22. Horse Lake

23. Range River

24. Fall Lake

25. Moose Lake (Fernberg Road)

26. Wood Lake

27. Snowbank Lake

29. North Kawishiwi River (Triangle Lake)

30. Lake One

31. Farm Lake

32. South Kawishiwi River

33. Little Gabbro L.

34. Island River

35. Isabella Lake

36. Hog Creek (Perent Lake)

37. Kawishiwi Lake

38. Sawbill Lake (and Alton Lake)

39. Baker Lake

40. Homer Lake

41. Brule Lake (and Juno Lake)

43. Bower Trout Lake (Lower Trout Lake)

44. Dislocation Lake (and Ram Lake, Rum Lake)

47. Lizz Lake (from Poplar Lake)

48. Meeds Lake (from Poplar Lake)

49. Skipper Lake (from Poplar Lake)

51. Ham Lake

52. Round Lake (and Missing Link Lake, Tuscarora Lake)

53. Brant Lake

54. Seagull Lake

55. Saganaga Lake

57. Magnetic Lake (from Gunflint Lake)

58. South Lake

60. Duncan Lake

61. Daniels Lake

62. Clearwater Lake

64. East Bearskin Lake

68. Pine Lake (from McFarland Lake)

69. East Pike Lake

70. Moose Lake (and Lilly Lake to Mountain Lake)

71. Canada

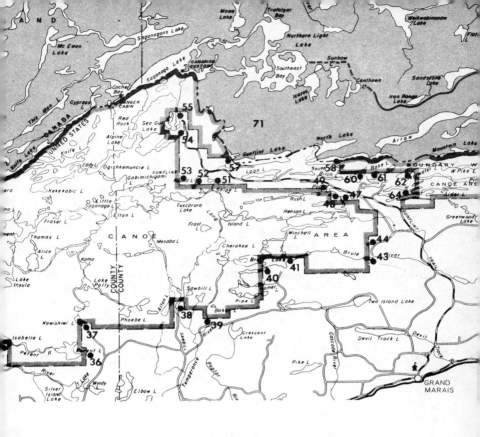

U. S. DEPARTMENT OF AGRICULTURE
FOREST SERVICE
John R. McGuire, Chief

BOUNDARY WATERS CANOE AREA
SUPERIOR NATIONAL FOREST

MINNESOTA
JANUARY 1977

SCALE

5   0   5   10   15 Miles

LEGEND

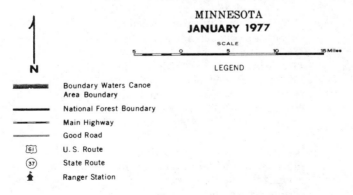

N

▬▬▬	Boundary Waters Canoe Area Boundary
———	National Forest Boundary
———	Main Highway
———	Good Road
🔲61	U. S. Route
⬤37	State Route
⚑	Ranger Station

Supervisor's Headquarters, Duluth, Minnesota

Regional Headquarters, Milwaukee Wisconsin

ABOUT THE AUTHOR

Marion Stresau is the author of several magazine articles and short stories about the lighter side of family life. Her first book, "Tomorrows Unlimited," is about her oldest daughter, who died in 1967. The book was published in 1973 by Branden Press, Boston.

She has lived with her husband, Dick, on a lake near Spooner, in northern Wisconsin, for about 18 years. A kayak, sailboat, and small outboard, designed and built by father and sons, started the family's boating interests. Canoes entered their lives in 1963 when their love affair with the Boundary Waters Canoe Area began.

ACKNOWLEDGMENTS

To Dick, my navigator, pathfinder and partner in all things, and to Steve, Mike, Dicky, Pat and Curt, who played important roles in our fun and adventures.

Also to Ann, my first "editor," to Dorothy, my first reader, and to Jackie and Marvin, Sandy, Lloyd and Hugh, Wendy, and Cliff, who gave time and encouragement along the way.

And to the Forest Service whose supervision and maintenance of the Boundary Waters Canoe Area made all these experiences possible.

Chapter 1
Paddling Blind

Principal Lakes: One, Two, Three, and Horseshoe

Not until the year of our 25th wedding anniversary had I ever set foot in a canoe—and then reluctantly, mainly to please my husband. But a spark of enthusiasm was lit that summer of 1963 which flared into a bonfire. From then on all our vacations were spent canoeing in the Boundary Waters Canoe Area of northern Minnesota.

We were lucky to live only 200 miles from this unique part of our country. Lying within the Superior National Forest, the BWCA unites at the Canadian border with the Quetico Provincial Park to form over 3000 square miles of roadless area interlaced with a labyrinth of connecting lakes. The most famous of these form the boundary chain extending 200 miles westerly from Lake Superior to International Falls, the fur trading route of the previous century known as the voyageur highway.

There is a constant struggle to preserve this historic wilderness. Overuse has become a serious problem with more than 150,000 visitors every summer. Trip permits have been required for several years and reservations are now necessary. Proponents for multiple use wage a continuing battle. In our 12 summers of paddling a few of the BWCA's 1200 miles of canoe routes, passing through or camping on 86 of its lakes, travelling the same portages used by the voyageurs and generations of Indians before them, we have become involved in the struggle.

But in July 1963 I knew little about the BWCA and, to be honest, couldn't have cared less. With our four older children all off on their own and our youngest, nine year old Steve, in summer camp, we had decided to celebrate our anniversary with a vacation trip. Just the two of us. I could picture it—a leisurely scenic drive, nice little country inn eating places, stops at plush motels. No meals to get; no work. Rest and relaxation all the way!

We hadn't quite made up our minds where we'd go although

1

the circle route around Lake Superior was most appealing. I was
dreaming over an advertising circular of North Shore motels one July
evening when my husband Dick strode in and slid a map of the
Superior National Forest in front of me.

"I've a great idea!" he said with a gleam in his eye. "How
about that wilderness canoe trip we used to talk about? The Boundary Waters Canoe Area is only a few miles off the circle route."

I'm afraid my mumbled response was anything but enthusiastic. The time we'd talked about it was way back before the children were born. What had seemed like a romantic adventure then
now sounded like plain hard work. And not a little scary. The
mere thought of sleeping with only a thin layer of fabric between
me and the great outdoors sent chills up my spine. My sense of
adventure seemed to have shrivelled to the size of a dried pea.

Nevertheless, in the end, when we decided on the circle
route, I consented to include Ely, Minnesota, a well known jumping
off place for BWCA canoe trips, as a stopover. Just to look around,
I made clear, fervently hoping there'd be no canoes available for
rent on short notice.

Then fate took a hand. I came across a magazine article
about a family that had taken a canoe trip in this area and had had
a great time, apparently with remarkable ease.

On impulse I followed the author's suggestion and wrote
to a canoe trip outfitter in Ely. A prompt personal reply followed
with an offer to help plan our trip. Intrigued, I began pouring over
the long lists of equipment and freeze dried foods, figuring out
what we'd need—just for fun, of course. Finally I stopped kidding
myself and boldly wrote for reservations for a two-day trip in
August. The next week I wrote again, increasing it to four days.
Only right to give it a fair trial.

I still had misgivings about my abilities as a canoeist or
camper but at least Dick had had experience—if you counted old
Boy Scout days. The truth was I was hooked; nothing could
dampen my enthusiasm by that time.

The drive to Ely could be described as scenic. We dined
in a nice little restaurant, but "plush" was hardly the word. for
the motel we stayed in. "Bare minimum" puts it more accurately.
A scarred oak double bed, bureau and chair were the only furnish-
ings in the small, uncarpeted room.

That evening as I surveyed the depressing jumble of camping equipment and food packets we'd picked up at the outfitters,
along with the camp clothes and sundry other items strewn across
the bed, I wondered what I'd let myself in for. Dick began stuffing

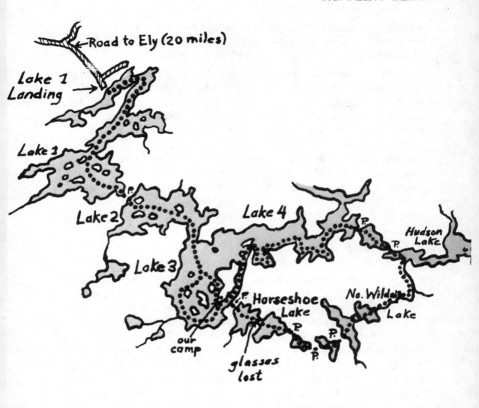

things enthusiastically into three dingy-looking canvas packs.

"Everything will work out great—you'll see," he said.

Uncomfortable on the hard chair, I watched in silence and made a solemn vow never again to get carried away by someone's glamorous description. It was one thing to read about adventure at home and quite another to find yourself in the midst of one.

A sunny morning and breakfast somewhat improved my outlook. With canoe cartopped, we drove about 20 miles to Lake One campground where we could park for a few days. The outfitter had suggested Lakes One, Two, Three and Four as a good beginner route. We could make a permanent camp on Lake Three and take a day trip, circling back through Lake Four. He had pointed out the route on the map.

Several people were gathered on the boat dock when we drove up. They were watching a party of three canoes paddling expertly out into the lake. Dick put our canoe in the water, tied it to the dock, and started transferring the packs. I prayed that everyone would leave before it came time to transfer myself down into the tiny front seat of the wobbling canoe.

No such luck. I'm sure it was obvious we were greenhorns and therefore good entertainment. Bits of friendly advice were offered and finally it came time to make my debut. Red-faced and trembling, I climbed unsteadily into the bow seat and managed a timorous farewell wave as we headed out into choppy water. The farther from shore we got the more our insecure craft bobbed and weaved in the waves. My knees began to shake in earnest and I could feel the thin aluminum sides shaking along with them. I was positive we were headed straight for the bottom. But there was no turning back now; the packs containing our livelihood were solidly ensconced in the bottom of the canoe and the group on the dock was still watching.

"Stop grabbing the paddle like a broomstick and you'll do a lot better," Dick called out.

His voice had a calming effect. I didn't even mind the overtone of amusement. Relaxing my death grip, I grasped the top of the paddle as directed. It was amazing how much easier it was. We were making progress toward a narrow end of the lake where the water was smoother. From there we seemed to almost glide the length of a twisting inlet, only to emerge into a much larger, rougher lake. All you could see was water, sky and tree-lined shores, a few islands dotting the distance. No houses. No signs. Nothing at all to indicate the direction to take. I began to see the need for the compass and detailed map Dick had gotten from the outfitter.

Checking both carefully, he set a course for the far end of the lake. Luck was with us. There was a strong wind at our backs; paddling was little more than steering. In about an hour we made it across to where the first portage should be. Dick headed for an opening in the dense shoreline brush. Sure enough, a small wooden sign announced a distance of 36 rods to the next lake. (A rod is about 5½ yards and 36 of them wasn't far, I was assured.) Getting to shore presented a problem with half-submerged rocks blocking the way. We came to a jarring halt a couple of times to the unnerving sound of aluminum scraping granite. Vigorous backpaddling freed us after much effort. Finally we made it.

With my ineffectual help Dick hauled out the packs, stacking them near the portage. Then he pulled the canoe up on shore. Hoisting it onto his shoulders with surprisingly little trouble, he started up the trail. I shoved my arms awkwardly into the wide straps of one of the packs and, grunting and twisting, somehow got the heavy thing on my back and staggered after him. Loose rocks on an uphill path made the going hard but it soon dropped steeply. Then keeping my balance became a problem. I could have sworn the pack had gained weight. At last the other lake came into view. I made it to the landing and dropped in a panting heap to the ground, feeling justifiably proud. But not for long. Dick had already started back. I struggled to my feet and followed.

Without the weight on my back there was a delicious lightness now to every step. For the first time I could look around at the deep shadowed forest—towering pines and leafy aspens forming a canopy overhead, lush green vegetation bordering the trail below. I breathed deeply, drinking in woodland smells, bird sounds, and the caressing coolness and feeling a part of the pristine beauty. For the moment "my cup runneth over!"

The return trip was much easier with Dick to help me get the pack on and to chat with on the way. We had made good time, he said. There was only a small lake and another short portage before we'd stop for lunch.

The canoe was loaded and we were ready to shove off when a couple travelling in the opposite direction paddled in for a landing. We pulled over to allow them room, exchanging small talk. They had a cabin near Ely, we found out, and were frequent canoe trippers in the BWCA. I was glad to note their age was close to ours. Everyone else we had met, or seen at a distance, appeared to be at least a decade or two younger. The woman was obviously a veteran camper. I felt quite the greenhorn, watching her lift an outsize pack up on her back as though it were filled with cotton candy. But what made my mouth drop open was seeing her hang it from her forehead by a strap (tumpline, I later learned) and set off up the rocky portage path at a lively dogtrot. Shades of the voyageurs!

We pulled in for lunch at a campsite on Lake Two. Perched on a rock ledge overlooking the lake, we munched sandwiches and fruit, sore muscles and tired backs forgotten. I was beginning to enjoy myself. There was a long paddle ahead, however. Dick pointed out that our route would take us the length of this lake plus some narrows before we came to Lake Three. We might have a long way to go there before finding a campsite. At least there were no more portages, for which I was devoutly thankful. My shoulders felt as though they had grooves worn in them from the pack straps.

By midafternoon we had come into Lake Three and were starting to look for a place to camp. Bare rocks with open spaces under the trees behind them usually turned out to be official campsites. These, I learned, came equipped with an iron grate for cook fires, a picnic table, and primitive sanitary facilities—consisting of a box in the woods at the end of a solitary trail, its lack of four walls made up for by scenic surroundings. One party to a campsite was the rule, although in those days any number to a party was allowed. (The party limit is now 10.) Hacking out your own campsite was not approved of, except in emergency, and would have been extremely difficult in the dense brush.

Having read that bears could be avoided by camping on islands, I made sure we investigated only island campsites. No problem, as there were many. However, the good ones all seemed to be occupied and most others were too small to afford privacy. I was getting discouraged when far down the lake we saw a long sweep of bare rock, tall pines cresting a ridge behind it. We put more effort into our paddling, though progress seemed to be by inches, and finally came close enough to see it was a good campsite; best of all, unoccupied. Up on the ridge a large boulder formed a natural back for the fire grate and the nearby picnic table commanded a spectacular view of the lake. Beneath the pines was a level place for a tent. A deluxe apartment couldn't have pleased me more!

Excitedly we lugged the packs up from the canoe and set to work, tiredness forgotten. Dick set up the tent while I unpacked and sorted gear. Glancing up once, I noticed a log pole nailed high between two tall slender pines. For hanging up your food pack at night to keep out bears, Dick explained.

Bears! In my delight over the campsite I hadn't given a thought to whether it was on an island or a peninsula. It's an island, Dick assured me, but the suggestion of a smile made me suspicious. Patiently he got out the map, showing me the place. It was an island all right—about a mile long by half mile wide. A whole family of bears could live on one this big! But it did come within my rules.

Bears or no bears, the truth was I wanted to stay. I couldn't imagine a nicer place. It wasn't until much later that I learned (what Dick had been careful not to mention) that bears are excellent swimmers As it turned out, I never gave bears another thought, sleeping soundly each night. Outdoor exercise and a comfortable air mattress were powerful sleeping potions.

The morning dawned bright and hot. We were up early, breakfasting on pancakes which we shared with feathered visitors—large gray jays, whiskey jacks or camp robbers as they're commonly called, freeloaders who knew all the tricks. They must have plied their trade around campsites for many seasons. Leave your plate unguarded even a second or two and you'd have to shoo a bright-eyed diner from your breakfast. The robber would leave in a protest of flapping wings, carrying off a last bite. But they were great entertainers and fun to watch. We soon learned to keep food covered, throwing tidbits for them to swoop down on or catch in midair.

Packing a lunch, we set out after breakfast on the circle route marked for us by the outfitter. It wound through small lakes named Horseshoe and North Wilder, then down a meandering stream, before crossing the upper half of Lake Four and back into Lake Three where our camp was. There were six short portages, which would only have to be crossed once with no packs. It sounded like an easy day's trip, as the outfitter had said.

Trouble began with the first portage. The map showed it around a point on the shore opposite our camp. Back and forth we paddled, peering into the dense brush. No sign of a portage anywhere. Finally Dick settled for the most open place. Shouldering the canoe, he pushed through foliage and over fallen logs on what once might have been a trail. Luckily we soon came out on the edge of what was obviously Horseshoe Lake.

Not until the following day did we discover that the portage, well travelled and in good condition, was almost directly across from our campsite. There was even a gnarled old cedar trunk leaning out over the water as a marker, if we'd only known. Lesson number one: don't put implicit trust in a map (although for the most part the Fisher maps sold at most outfitters are excellent.) We had yet to discover geological survey maps, dependable for accuracy and topographical detail, which became indispensable on future trips.

As we glided out into calm waters I stopped paddling, leaning back to absorb the wildness and beauty. Deep green conifers with patches of red-tinged rocks edged the azure lake. No sign of humanity anywhere. A gentle breeze tempered the heat of the blazing sun. I pulled a tube of suntan cream out of my pocket and applied it liberally before tossing it back to Dick. Taking off his glasses, he slipped them into his shirt pocket so he could rub cream over his face. Then we headed for a narrow passage that divided the lake into its horseshoe shape. Resting paddles, we slid silently through. Or almost.

A sudden roar of dismay shattered the quiet. I jerked around to see Dick peering over the side of the canoe, an expression of utter disbelief on his face. He had flipped off his shirt, he said, and somewhere down there were his glasses! Extremely nearsighted, without them he'd be lost.

We'd be lost!

Beaching the canoe on a rock ledge, he peeled off clothes and jumped in. "Lucky it's shallow here," he called confidently.

A half hour or so later Dick had retrieved several sticks and an old beer can—but no glasses. There was a current running through the narrow passage, which had probably carried them off into deep water by now. It was hopeless.

"Don't worry. We'll find our way. Simple matter of reading the map and checking the shoreline." He said this in an effort to console me.

"But I can't read maps and you can't see the shoreline!" I wailed.

"We'll hug shore so I can. No problem."

He was right—as long as we travelled through the small lakes, over portages, and down the narrow stream. We lunched on a little island, swam in the refreshing lake, and enjoyed ourselves immensely. The problems began when we entered large, multi-inleted Lake Four. Water seemed to stretch endlessly ahead, nearby points of land offering only confusion. We headed out into the lake for a better view.

It was a struggle making progress against the sizable waves, whipped by winds we'd barely noticed on the small lakes. When it began to get frighteningly rough, Dick stopped paddling to study the map. The canoe bobbed and wallowed around. I shifted my paddle from side to side in an unsuccessful attempt to steady it from the bow.

"Hurry up and start paddling!" I yelled.

"Look for a point of land on the left with an island to the right," he called back, ignoring my frantic cries. "Do you see the island?"

I'd forgotten my eyes had to serve the two of us. "No. . . Yes—Yes, I do!" I shouted. I wasn't sure it was an island but at that point I was ready to build one to get him to pick up his paddle. Finally I felt the forward thrust of the canoe from behind and breathed easier.

"According to the map there's a narrow passage behind the next point that will take us back to Lake Three," Dick explained.

It took a half hour's paddling to find out that he was wrong. We had come into a dead end inlet. Nor was the next point the right one; or the next, though we paddled hopefully down the far side of each.

"If I could just see the shoreline," Dick groaned. "I know it's here somewhere."

But supposing it wasn't, I thought, with the beginnings of panic. There were no signposts; no route numbers.

"Let me see the map," I said, trying to keep fear out of my voice. I might as well have looked at a map of the moon. It seemed to me we could be in any one of hundreds of lakes.

"Maybe we're lost," I gasped.

"No, we're not lost. A person is lost only when he panics. We're simply confused," he said matter-of-factly. "The passage is probably around the next point."

I was positive he was wrong but glad to grab at any straw, even his flimsy optimism. By now every muscle I owned, including some I'd never known about, was protesting. Blisters were rubbed raw on both hands. My skin, despite doses of suntan cream, was on fire. I marvelled that I could keep going. But there was no stopping. No matter how many dead end inlets we struggled in and out of, we had to find our camp.

It was after five by now and we were hungry, having foolishly eaten all our lunch and thrown remaining crumbs to chipmunks. At least we had plenty of water to drink by simply dipping a cup over the side in these unpolluted lakes. As we rounded the next point I saw campers on a clearing around a cook fire. One man was near shore chopping wood.

"Can you tell me what lake this is?" I called out.

He glanced up. "Lake Four," he said.

My heart sank. After all this paddling I figured we must have somehow come into Lake Three. Miserably I blurted out that we were lost and couldn't find our campsite.

"That's bad." He shook his head and turned back to chopping.

I was ready to cry.

"Bet this is the right inlet; our camp is down at the end," Dick said.

His optimism no longer helped. My arms kept on lifting and dipping mechanically but I had given up. Then, way up ahead my eye caught sight of something vaguely familiar. A gnarled trunk was leaning out from a banking at a peculiar angle. Suddenly I knew. The old trunk was across from our campsite at the portage entrance! No voyageur returning to his homeland from years on the trail could have known greater joy at that moment.

We were both exhausted when at last we reached shore and crawled up the steep path. A fire and one-pot meal were managed before we climbed wearily into sleeping bags. It's surprising what a sound night's sleep will do We had planned the next day in camp "licking our wounds," expending only enough energy to cook and eat. But by midafternoon we were out in the canoe again, making sure to keep to the familiar end of our lake.

Breakfasting with our cheerful gang of jays on the final morning, we were dallying over a second cup of coffee, reluctant to start breaking camp. I became aware of something black and shiny at the edge of the clearing. Peering intently, I discovered it was an eye belonging to a snowshoe rabbit. In his brown summer coat he blended so perfectly with the pine needles and brush that he had gone unnoticed. I motioned to Dick and we sat very still. The rabbit seemed to sense an invitation and ventured a few hops in our direction, then sat up to test the air with his wiggling nose. We didn t move an eyelash. Ears erect, he hopped toward us again, stopping once to nibble at a small green sprig.

In the course of the next five or ten minutes he kept shortening the distance between us until he was almost at our feet. Dick and I exchanged smiles of amazement. Slowly I stretched out my hand with a crust of bread, letting it slip to the ground. In a moment or two he gathered courage to hop close enough to inspect it. Then, insulted with the quality of our breakfast, he drew back. In a flash he had disappeared in the brush.

More reluctant than ever to leave, we finally set about the business of packing up. When we shoved off we found the wind now shifted and at our backs again. It was hard to believe our luck. The trip back wasn't easy, however, with Dick's limited vision causing some mistakes and extra paddling now and then. When at last we pulled up at the Lake One landing dock, my "canoe muscles" were protesting loudly, my hands wore several bandaids, and my complexion rivalled an overripe tomato. With it all I had had a wonderful time.

Before we left Ely we bought a large book, "Superior-Quetico Canoe Maps"—14,500 square miles, covering the Superior National Forest in Minnesota and the Quetico Provincial Park in Ontario, it said on the cover. Based on the area we'd covered in four days, Dick figured it would take us over a thousand years to explore the rest of it. With no realistic ideas of accomplishing that, we did expect to return next summer. There was no doubt about it—we were hooked!

Chapter 2
Up the Wall

Principal Lakes: Seagull, Ogishkemuncie, and Ester

Looking back on it later, we suspected the stage had been deliberately set to hook us that first trip. Never since have we experienced such perfect weather; the wind at our backs the whole time. Perhaps it was the Mamaygwessey, legendary gremlins of the Cree Indians. These little beings inhabit the rocks around rapids and streams of the northern lakes, according to Sigurd Olson, who writes of them in "The Lonely Land." When canoes pass through, they delight in grasping paddles or gunwales, laughing with glee when a canoe tips over. There's no malice in their antics, no real harm done, just good clean fun. I could imagine them lurking in the narrows of Horseshoe Lake, highly entertained by the episode of the lost glasses. Had they influenced the elements on our behalf to entice us back for future targets? There were times we could believe it!

Our second canoe trip, in the summer of 1964, began in direct contrast to the first as far as weather was concerned. Listening to the swish of wiper blades and catching glimpses of dark gray water through the trees, as we slowly bumped our way along a potholed wilderness road, I found old doubts creeping back. What was I doing here, about to expose myself to the vagaries of the elements and become a slave to primitive living when I could be relaxing in comfort at home? The hours spent last winter dreaming over outfitters' mail order catalogues and poking around camping equipment stores had always been accompanied by visions of sunny skies and sparkling lakes. Even our day's journey to Ely in May to pick out a secondhand canoe and various equipment items had been bright and full of promise for the vacations to come. Rain simply hadn't entered my mind—at least not a steady downpour, leaden-sky variety on takeoff day.

"Rain before seven, clear before eleven," Dick quoted with undampened enthusiasm.

"That gives it just 13 minutes," I said dourly, consulting my watch.

He tried a different tack. "How about driving up to that resort beyond Seagull Lake for lunch? Should have cleared up by the time we get back."

I was positive it was an all-day rain but readily agreed. We were travelling the Gunflint Trail, a narrow gravel road winding up some 50 miles northeast into the border lakes from the small Lake Superior town of Grand Marais. (The road is now black-topped most of the way, construction work having begun that summer.) Our plans were for a 10-day canoe trip from Seagull Lake, a popular takeoff point near the end of Gunflint Trail with a public parking lot and a boat ramp. We had mapped out a circle route of 14 lakes and a dozen connecting portages, about 40 miles in all, which would allow a leisurely pace with stopover days now and then.

By the time we had eaten a passable lunch of canned soup and hamburgers in the rustic lodge's nearly empty dining room and had searched out a small grocery store for a few additions to our food supplies, it was well after two. To my surprise (but not Dick's) it had stopped raining and a pale sun was struggling to shine through openings in the clouds. Loading the canoe at the landing, we made a lucky last minute decision to pull out a tarp and rain gear, just in case.

My spirits rose as we paddled down a sheltered inlet, through brief rapids, and out into a wide expanse of lake. As far as we could see we had it all to ourselves. It wasn't long, however, before the sky darkened again and a threatening cloud sent us paddling fast toward shore. Pulling on ponchos and covering the packs, we waited out a brief hard shower. As soon as it stopped we set forth again, only to be followed by another storm cloud and repeat performance. At this rate it would be evening before we covered the five miles to the end of the lake.

When we had made it across an open bay and abreast of an island with a campsite, my aching arms were crying out at every dip of the paddle. I didn't care whether it was a good camp or not, only that it was unoccupied. Might not be a bad idea to stop here, I suggested, knowing full well the plans were to portage through to the next lake. With far less protest than I had anticipated (probably his muscles were sore too), Dick agreed.

The tent was barely set up before it rained again, this time the cats and dogs variety. Shoving packs inside, we scrambled in after them and tied shut the storm flap. Our nylon house met the test; we stayed nicely dry. During the next let-up, rain dripping from the trees, we managed a half-hearted fire and some watery stew. Before bedtime a crimson sky gave hope for clearing weather. We put the canoe in the water for a quiet paddle around our island, the silence suddenly shattered by four or five laughing, yodeling loons skidding in for landings on the pink mirror lake.

I climbed into my sleeping bag that night, greatly cheered, and was soon asleep. But not for long. It seemed only minutes later I was awakened by a thunderous commotion. An elephant galloping past the tent couldn't have made more noise. . . A bear? Heart pounding, I prodded Dick awake. The beast could be heard rummaging among a pile of cans in back. (Cans and bottles are now outlawed in the BWCA, I'm happy to say.) Just a r'coon or a skunk, Dick assured me sleepily, slipping back at once into snoring oblivion. Such was not my lot. Whatever was out there kept running around all night; or maybe there were several taking turns. With the food pack hung high in a tree. I knew there was no cause for worry about animals coming into the tent. Nevertheless, I got little sleep.

We awoke to a dark foggy morning, last night's promise a false one. Everything inside the tent was damp with condensation; everything outside was soggy and dripping. I thought longingly of my warm bed in a dry house. A kitchen with all the conveniences. A bathroom! But like it or not, here I was and much had to be done before we could leave this place—only to paddle off into a bleak lake with no idea where we'd find our next shelter.

Coffee and pancakes helped but the job of breaking camp was pretty terrible. Dampness added bulk and stuffing our gear into the three packs was a time-consuming, discouraging job. We still had a bucketful left over to carry on the portages. Our brand new lightweight packs, largest listed in the bargain mail order catalogue, were bursting at the seams, straps barely straining into the last holes. (We later learned this was a bad investment as the straps soon broke. The sturdy Duluth packs we replaced them with are still in good shape.) I felt as though I'd already put in a day's work when about an hour and a half later we nosed the canoe out from shore, mist wetting our faces and making the paddle handles slippery.

Ahead of us were four portages and three lakes if we were to reach Ogishkemuncie Lake, destination for the night. The first portage, 104 rods, more than double the length of the others, I had dreaded. But it turned out to be a paved road compared to some we'd tackled the year before. During our lunch stop at the far end of the first lake the sun came out, bright and hot. Things were

looking up. I dug out the map, more or less intelligible now since the hours spent over it last winter, and saw we had covered almost half the distance. The remaining portages were only a few black dots long and the lakes small blue ovals. An easy afternoon's trip!

It turned out I had a lot to learn about maps. Neat little dotted lines under my finger were something else again under my feet. The portages were the worst we'd ever encountered, steeper, rockier and puddled with black mud from recent rains. Toting the canoe and gear, and loading and unloading in mudholes was exhausting. Even so we weren't unaware of the primitive beauty and, on the steepest and rockiest portage, of the accompaniment of musical rapids and a waterfall in a trailside stream.

With an incredible feeling of relief we shoved the canoe from shore the last time and slid out into the smooth waters of Ogish Lake (as we later learned it was called). A mile or so of paddling and we passed through narrows, emerging into a wide basin. There had been no sign of open places to camp but far ahead appeared an island with a bare sweep of rock down to the water's edge, characteristic of campsites in this glacial terrain. It turned out to be a good one and all ours.

Dick, admitting to a tired back and sore shoulders as well as I, readily agreed to a day's stopover. I don't know whether animals ran around our tent that night or not—or any night after that. I slept much too soundly to hear them. What luxury to loll in our sleeping bags as long as we felt like it the next morning. Swimming and exploring around the island occupied us until lunch. In the afternoon Dick paddled across to a shrubby hillside in search of blueberries while I sunbathed on warm rocks. He was back earlier than I'd expected, holding forth a plastic pail full of fat, ripe berries. "We picked the right time—bushes are loaded. Blueberry tarts for supper!" he announced.

On canoe trips Dick not only assumes the role of chief cook but culinary artist as well, taking pride in concocting tasty treats from whatever is at hand. His tarts were fashioned out of biscuit mix pressed into tin cups and filled with sweetened berries. Aluminum foil folded into a three sided lean-to and placed on a flat rock in front of the campfire served as oven. Keeping the fire roaring hot was the trick, he claimed, adding sticks and blowing on it at frequent intervals. Clouds of ashes billowed up, some of which settled back down on the oven contents. But it didn't matter. As with almost everything else we ate around a campfire, flavors far surpassed anything at home. Steaming cups of thick pea soup, browned potato pancakes, coffee and the delectable tarts added up to a gourmet meal that night.

16

We set off in fine fettle the following morning, eager to get on with our trip. There was about a mile's paddling to a short portage into Jean Lake. At the end of Ogish a couple of men were breaking camp on a piney ridge above us, the first people we'd seen during our stay.

The portage trail between the lakes was easy but the take-off point on the other side, or lack of one, presented problems. Rocks dotted a shallow, muddy bay. Hoisting the canoe to his shoulders, Dick stepped cautiously from one wobbly foothold to another. Ahead was a solid-looking flat rock, just above water. Working his way out slowly, he got one foot planted and was bringing the other forward when the treacherous rock tilted. Dick fell backwards with a tremendous splash, the canoe crashing beside him. He came up mud-covered and spluttering mad but unhurt. The canoe had not fared as well, a large dent on its side where metal had met granite. No breaks, however; Dick soon had it pounded back in shape with his fist.

"Lucky thing it was the canoe and not me," he said, rubbing the damaged area reflectively. "Aluminum is lots more durable than flesh."

With no longer a reason to keep dry, he loaded the packs easily and helped me to a safe boarding spot; then retired to the woods for a quick change. A bath would have to wait.

"You know, I've got a sneaking suspicion the Mamay-gwessey were around," I said as we paddled out into clear water.

"Sure had all the earmarks," Dick laughed.

Ahead of us were two short portages with a small lake between before we tackled a long paddle down South Arm Knife Lake. While carrying gear over the second portage, we met a party of 10- to 12- year-olds and their youthful counselors, a camp name printed across their T-shirts. The trail soon became hazardous with weaving canoes, lurching packs and running boys. Like going the wrong direction on a freeway. We decided to wait out the traffic, pulling our canoe and packs as far off the beaten track as possible. Comfortably resting on a log, we watched three more canoes come in, boys leaping unconcernedly into water at least calf deep before they reached the landing. All wore stout leather hiking boots.

"That's the way the Indians did it, protecting fragile bark canoes from the rocks," Dick commented. "They're getting a history lesson."

History lesson or not, it was a good thing their mothers couldn't see this, I thought. No doubt these same sons had been admonished many times not to get their feet wet—and only in puddles, at that!

Munching cheese sandwiches high on a windy ledge above South Arm Knife Lake, we watched a party of four canoes below struggling to make progress against strong wind and waves, congratulating ourselves on our good luck to be travelling in the opposite direction. After lunch we fairly flew down the long northeast arm of the lake, coasting into an inlet where a sign announced that it was 120 rods to Hanson Lake. It was four times longer than any portage that morning but at least it was the last. One more lake and a paddle-through stream would take us into Ester Lake, our destination.

Two canoes were pulled up at the landing. While we were unloading four people emerged from the trail. "You might as well turn back," one of the women called out. "We just hiked in to take a look and it's the steepest trail you've ever seen—believe me!"

The man beside her nodded. "No way to get a canoe up."

The other man rubbed a hand over his beard. "Well, maybe if each of them takes an end—one pushes and the other pulls. . .I don't know."

I glanced sideways at Dick, knowing the longer they discussed it the more irresistible the challenge to him. As for my taking an end of the canoe, that was out. After one disastrous trial he had labeled me worse than useless. I kept weaving and throwing him off balance, he complained.

Thanking the people politely, Dick got the canoe up on his shoulders and set off up the trail. "We'll give it a try," he said.

There was nothing to do but follow. I heaved a pack up on my back, not too ungracefully, I hoped, and hurried after him, catching glimpses of "they'll find out" expressions, as I turned to wave.

"Maybe we'd better go back," I shouted to Dick as soon as I caught up.

"Can't. Got a circle of lakes to make. This is the only way through," he hollered from under the canoe.

I knew it was useless to argue. In any case, the steep path needed my undivided attention. Then all at once I found myself confronted with a wall. It rose up almost vertically about 50 feet. A trail of sorts went up it which no mountain goat in his right mind would attempt—let alone a two-legged being with a canoe on his head! Dick, having leaned the canoe against a "rest" (strategically placed cross beams nailed high in trees along hard portages), was silently surveying the cliff. Before I could gather my wits to argue, he had shouldered the canoe and started up.

Slowly, one carefully placed foothold after another, he made it to the top without a stop. To this day I'll never know how he did it. Not daring to look up, I followed, using hands as well as feet, struggling to keep my balance under the unwieldy pack. Twice I had to grab a desperate hold on a rock or branch with the terrifying sensation that I was about to topple over backwards. When at last I had clawed my way to the top I found Dick sprawled on the ground, red-faced and panting, the canoe propped nearby. I dropped where I was, not even removing the pack.

We rested a long time before returning for the other gear and decided to get everything up over the rock wall before continuing. Whatever lay ahead had to be easier, we reassured each other. But we were far from through the ordeal. The trail wound up narrowly beside deep ravines, then down through boggy places where we squished into spongy moss with each step. It was slow going. As it had to be traversed three times in all, the afternoon was well used up when we finally emerged at Hanson Lake for the last time. We would have been glad to settle for the nearest campsite but found none, as we wearily paddled the length of the lake.

Arriving at the outlet stream, we found it choked with marsh grass and blocked by a beaver dam. Unloading and loading was more than I could bear to think about. But Dick said the solution was easy. All we had to do was climb out on the banks and slide the canoe over. He was right.

Luckily we didn't have far to go on Ester Lake before coming upon a campsite at the far end of an island. It didn't have a beach and was too sheltered to get any breezes but at that point any place to pitch a tent looked like heaven to me.

We climbed into our sleeping bags before dark that evening, more than ready for a night's rest. But in spite of sore muscles, bruises and scrapes neither of us felt overtired or exhausted. We must be getting in trim, I recorded proudly in my journal.

"Sure would help if maps showed ups and downs," I sighed before dozing off. "Then at least we'd be prepared."

"What we need are topographical maps. Meant to get one," Dick agreed sleepily.

Just how great the need we were soon to find out. If I'd ever known what lay in store for us on the next portage, I think I'd have been tempted to spend the rest of my life on Ester Lake.

Chapter 3
Maps, Mistakes, and Moosetracks

Principal Lakes: Ester, Ashdick, and Swamp

We woke to a still, hot morning, the tent becoming uncomfortable with the first slanting rays of the sun. A good day to spend in camp, I suggested, with muddy clothes to be washed and baths needed. Dick agreed wholeheartedly, though not for spending in camp, I suspected, after seeing his eyes light up the night before when he'd pointed out cliffs across the lake. "Bet there's blueberries up there," he'd said. But it wasn't just the berries, I knew. Cliffs are to be climbed—simply because, like mountains, they're there. The lake was there too—wild, big, extending as far north as we could see through the binoculars. Dick was an explorer at heart and opportunity was knocking.

By 10 o'clock we had wrung out the last piece of wash and hung it to dry on tent ropes and convenient bushes. With a lunch pail of peanut butter sandwiches, dried fruit, chocolate and lemonade mix stowed in the canoe along with towels, soap and a change of clothing, we were off. There was only a gentle breeze that did little to cool as we headed out into the wide part of the lake. Dick set a course in the direction of the cliffs a mile or so away. Must be 200 feet high, he estimated, his interest growing by leaps and bounds.

Mine was growing too but not in the cliffs—even the first dozen steps on a lookout tower has me scared to look down. My eye was on a small peninsula jutting into the lake just this side of the cliffs. Tall pines offered shade and a rock beach slanted down to the water, perfect for swimming, sunning and drying hair. At our campsite the rocks were steep, moss covered, and slippery underwater. Worst of all, we'd found big leeches clinging to them. Former campers had dumped pot scrapings and discarded fish parts in the shallow water near the landing, attracting these repulsive little scavengers. It was a lesson to us. After that we burned all garbage in a hot fire.

Paddling in close, we found the smooth rock slab extended a long way out under clear water, no moss or sign of leeches. If people had camped here it had been long enough ago to erase all evidence.

Staccato raucous crowing caught our attention. A black bird, larger and rougher-shaped than a crow, was slowly circling the cliffs; then made a detour in our direction, screeching guttural insults.

"It's a raven. . . Do you think he's saying 'Nevermore'?" Dick asked.

"I think he's telling us to leave—and in strong language," I replied.

The canoe scraped slowly onto rock and I climbed out with lunch pail and paraphernalia, heading up to the shady grove. With scarcely a backward glance, Dick shoved off, paddling across the narrow inlet toward the rocky base of the cliffs. He'd be back for lunch. I searched out a comfortable spot, open to breeze and a view, a sturdy pine for a backrest. I had brought along my log book, planning to catch up while he was gone.

In an hour or so I heard the canoe returning. Dick met me, pockets bulging with fat ripe berries—he'd forgotten to take the pail. It had been a rough climb but worth it, he said. From the top he'd had a view of Ester Lake as though looking down on a map; lakes in the distance were recognizable. There was no sign of another campsite, boat, or people anywhere. Nothing but wilderness as far as you could see.

"Halloo!" we shouted across the lake.

"Halloo!" the cliff answered. We were the last man and woman on earth, we laughed. A strange, heady feeling. Exciting! For 48 hours, from the time we left South Arm Knife Lake until we arrived at Swamp Lake the following afternoon, we saw no one.

Sweaty, with scratches and bruises from his climb, Dick was eager for a swim. He headed down the rock slope, pulling off clothes as he went. Grabbing towels and soap, I followed. We stayed in the water a long time. For unqualified enjoyment it's hard to beat swimming in a clear wilderness lake on a hot day— unencumbered by a swimsuit!

It was a do-as-we-please day: a nap in the shade after lunch; then a leisurely paddle back to camp, stopping on the way for a glimpse of Rabbit Lake which Dick had seen from the cliff. The portage was only 16 rods but had had little recent use. We climbed over rocks, skirted overhanging trees, and leaped a stream that meandered back and forth across the trail, thankful we hadn't brought along the canoe.

The laundry was nicely dry on our return; the campsite hot, breezeless, and infested with biting black flies. Bug spray had little effect. As soon as the supper dishes were washed and Dick had chopped a pile of wood for our breakfast fire, we retreated to our tent with plans for waking with the sun and getting an early morning start.

It was early when we awakened—but not with the sun. Rolls of thunder shook the rock base of our island, growing louder. Rain was soon coming down like a spigot had been opened; lightning flashed and thunder exploded. We scrambled to tie shut door and window flaps and pull the packs away from tent walls, thankful we'd had the foresight to bring them inside. The food box, roped in a tree, was always covered with a "trash baggie" to protect it from bugs and birds. Burrowing back into the soft luxury of sleeping bags, we fell asleep again.

Our second awakening was to a rhythmic tattooing on our nylon ceiling. The watch showed something after seven. Summoning enough energy to poke our heads out the door, we surveyed a gray, wet world. Whether it was still raining or not was hard to tell under the dripping trees. Dick dressed and crawled outside to get the fire going. We were organized on travel mornings. My role: stuffing our clothes into plastic bags, pulling out mattress plugs (to start them deflating), rolling up sleeping bags, and packing the small canvas tote bag with our personal items. By the time I was dressed and had carried an armload down to the picnic table Dick had the fire going, the food box out of the tree, and was sorting out breakfast stuff. At least that's the way we planned it.

This morning I came down the trail to find a scowling husband bent over a small pile of wet kindling, an anemic trickle of smoke curling up; the food pack still high in the tree.

"Forgot to cover the wood," he growled.

Our careful chain of preparations had been broken by our weakest link—forgetting. And it would have been so easy to slip the wood inside a baggie the night before!

Birch bark makes an excellent fire starter--the sad sight of peeled birches around every campsite attests to that! I hurried into the woods to search for logs and fallen birches. It wasn't long before I had collected a good handful of bark. Even wet, the white papery curls caught at once, giving a steady blaze. But the soaked wood refused to cooperate. The morning was half gone before Dick finally managed a fire hot enough to boil water for our long-awaited coffee. The blueberry pancakes, needing high heat, were not the best, but with brown sugar and margarine they tasted wonderful anyway. We ate hungrily, then set about cleaning up and breaking camp. Clouds still darkened the sky but the rain had stopped. It was noon before we shoved off.

The day's trip was mapped out taking the trail from Ester's northernmost tip over to Ottertrack and then on to Swamp, both border lakes on the voyageur highway. It included two portages about 90 rods each and roughly three miles of paddling before a "lift-over" into Big Sag where we planned to camp. Plans changed at the first portage when we hiked in a short distance and discovered a hill to rival "the wall"—in steepness if not in height. Dick pointed out another route we could take, a half mile back on Ester to a 45-rod trail over to Caribou, then to Swamp through a small in-between lake. The lengths of these last two portages weren't given on the map but didn't look bad. No sense climbing a steep trail if there was a way around. We were learning—or so we thought!

We found the portage where it was supposed to be but the sign said Ashdick Lake. Up and down, near shore, we paddled searching for Caribou. Confused and frustrated, we finally gave up. This had to be it, whatever the name. (Later we discovered the lake named Ashdick on every map but ours!) It was a miserable swampy trail but at least had no hills of any consequence. There was about a mile to the other end of Ashdick where the portage to Swamp Lake began. With no way of knowing how many rods were ahead of us—the map showed a straight line, which should have made us suspicious!—we decided to make a quick lunch stop at the top of a steep bank, only open place on the thickly wooded shores.

Paddling on afterwards, we noticed the treeline rising high on the right, indicating a steep hill where the trail should be—an unsettling thought. But there was no portage. Anywhere. For the second time that day we inched our way up and down the wide basin at the lake's end searching for an opening in the brush. It was excruciating. On the map the portage was plainly marked. Too late to go back; there had to be a way through. Dick chose a spot where the treeline was lowest and a tiny inlet went in under an overhanging bush. Paddling as hard as we could while bent low, ducking branches, we forced the canoe in and suddenly found ourselves in an open swampy area. Beyond was a hill and, to our immense relief, the semblance of a trail. The portage! A long way from the place shown on the map but it had to be.

We pulled the canoe up onto spongy ground and were picking our way across the swamp, looking for the firmest footing, when we stopped in amazement. Ahead of us, half mired in mud, was an aluminum flat-bottomed boat! Obviously it had been there some time. Where were its owners? Would we come upon their remains on the trail, we joked a little nervously. Or had they abandoned it because the portage was too bad to get it over?

There wasn't time to speculate; whatever the answer, a hard trek lay ahead. We unloaded and piled the packs at the base of a towering tree, driest spot we could find, and Dick started off with the canoe. Squishing my way from hummock to hummock with a pack on my back, arms clutching paddles, lunch pail and assorted extras, I found the mosquitoes; or they found me. There had been a few and then all at once clouds of them. Signals had been sent out: come one, come all—succulent, tender humans! Join in the feast. They came as though they hadn't eaten in months, zooming in on arms, legs, face, siphoning up seven course meals while I approached near hysteria in my helplessness.

As soon as my feet hit solid ground I threw down my armload and grabbed a can of bug spray. How sweet to see them drop! I sprayed all exposed skin till I was dripping, then hurried to catch up with Dick. Mosquitoes he looks on as a minor annoyance, even when they're biting, seldom bothering to swat or brush them away. If I'm around they leave him alone anyway. But not this time. His arms, neck and face were black with them. Gratefully he put down the canoe and let me spray him head to foot.

We crossed the swamp again to bring over the other packs before tackling the trail. Bug can in hand, I backpacked the second time well fortified but the whining, hungry mob followed close, zeroing in on any spot I'd overlooked.

Dick set his pack down beside the other and stood staring back across the swamp. "Never saw white cedars so big—that one where we stacked the packs must be 300 years old!"

I grunted and kept going. To stand still was an open invitation to the freeloaders. How he could marvel over trees at a time like this was beyond me.

The narrow path led up a rocky ridge, then flattened out and wound through dense brush. In some places I pushed through waist-high overgrowth; fallen trees had to be climbed over or under, impossible to circumvent in the thick tangle. Down again and the portage turned into a muddy track across another swamp. The sun now shining through the leafy canopy above was turning out jungle humidity. Bug spray had lost its effect, even though I was on a second can. Finally it dawned on me that I was sweating it off faster than I could spray it on! I gave up—the mosquitoes were winning anyway—and concentrated on moving at a quicker pace.

MAPS, MISTAKES AND MOOSETRACKS

Once again the tortuous trail wound up a steep rise. I panted on, sliding on loose rocks. Around a bend; down again; up again; path barely visible through the underbrush; bushes meeting overhead, scratching my face, scraping the pack. Would it ever end? Another bend and it did. The trunk of a fallen tree, as big around as a telephone pole, lay squarely across the trail. It was too high off the ground and thickly branched to get the canoe over or under, trailside brush too dense to go around it. I dropped my pack and retraced steps to meet Dick, swatting as I went in a purely reflex action. Going back after coming this far was unthinkable but continuing on, even if we did get the canoe through, could be worse.

To Dick the decision was already made. We would go on. Satisfying himself that he could not carry, slide or shove the canoe over or around the tree, he propped it at one side, dug the Sven folding saw out of a pack, and set to work. Rather then endure a mosquito-plagued rest, I backtracked to bring up one of the packs. By the time I returned Dick had sawed a piece out of the tree and had the canoe almost pushed through sideways.

"Going back for the other pack," he said, leaning the canoe against the trunk on the other side.

I dropped my load beside it. "I may still be here when you come back," I moaned.

With my bandanna neckerchief I wiped arms, hands and face, applying bug spray lavishly. Then I sank down, leaning against the pack, reveling in the still, brief respite. All too soon the pests were back, hovering, humming, daring each other to be the first to light. I struggled to my feet, forcing arms through pack straps. No sense sitting there, offering cafeteria service. I would keep going until I reached the lake this time—couldn't be much farther.

The trail continued straight, easy hiking for a short distance. A sharp turn and it began to drop, the ground growing mushier with each step until I was picking my way in oozy mud, trying to avoid water-filled holes. Something strange about those holes, I thought—round-shaped, evenly spaced. Firmer ground suddenly gave me the answer. Before my astonished eyes was a moose track--big as a dinner plate! (Or so it seemed to me.) Not just one; several, far enough apart to indicate a very large animal with a long stride. The tracks looked so fresh I glanced around nervously, half expecting to see the huge creature watching me.

All at once I felt very alone and very frightened. Stashing my pack in the bushes, I fled back to Dick as fast as I could go. A tree blocking the trail was one thing but an angry moose (and how did I know he wouldn't be?) was quite another!

CANOEING THE BOUNDARY WATERS

When I reached the propped canoe Dick was just coming into view from the other direction. Though skeptical, he found my moose tracks of interest but nothing to worry about.

"They're shy of people—you'd never meet one on the trail," he assured me.

Nevertheless, I was glad to follow close behind when we started down the portage. He had exchanged his pack for the canoe, planning to get it across the boggy place before returning for the pack. I had exchanged loads too, now toting my "favorite," the lightweight pack with clothing and sleeping bags, which I alternated with the medium-weight, mattresses and cooking pots. The third, a heavyweight containing tent and food box, I was glad to leave exclusively to Dick.

We had learned that alternating loads to stopping points (called posés, a French word meaning rest, by the voyageurs) along the trail was less tiring than carrying straight through, giving muscles a chance to rest. Veteran canoe trippers and outfitters recommend this method on all long portages.

As soon as we had made it past the mud and water holes onto firmer ground, Dick set the canoe down—no convenient "rests" on this trail—and went back to examine the tracks. No doubt in his mind. It was a moose all right, a big one—must have passed through here in the last hour or so. Breaking off a stick, he estimated the depth of the holes. The animal had sunk down 10 or 12 inches while our tracks in the same place were only two to three inches deep!

I now had a choice: hike back with Dick, although both my packs were here; wait with the mosquitoes until he returned; or backpack ahead. The only sensible decision was to go on. Determining not to think about the moose, I swapped packs—get the heaviest over with first—and started off. It seemed to me we must have hiked twice the distance on the map already; I should come out at the small lake any minute.

Twenty minutes later I was still plodding on, rounding each bend expectantly, driven by one desire—to get there. I held mental pictures of a lake through the trees, collapsing gratefully on the ground, blessed relief to weary legs and aching shoulders. Rest! But not before I made it. Starting again would be too hard.

The trail began climbing—a bad sign; lakes are in low places. A sharp turn and I was staring at a rock ledge above me, the path straight up. No way around. More than I could manage-- but my legs kept going. Slipping and staggering under the awkward pack, I grabbed for handholds on rocks and scrawny bushes. Just above was a small scrub oak, sturdy enough to get a good grip on. I reached up, leaning sideways, and the pack lurched, throwing me completely off balance. There was no way to keep from falling. Down I went, sliding backwards, belly-bumping on loose rocks to the bottom. I didn't even try to get up. The end had come. At least I'd die giving the hungry hordes of mosquitoes a treat.

How long I lay there, not moving, I don't know—my memory blurs thinking about it. The next thing I recall is the sound of footsteps; a strong hand sliding under my packstrap, lifting. With this support I found I could scramble to my feet and keep moving. Together we made it to the top, not talking, every ounce of energy needed for the job at hand. The ordeal over, we found a ledge of rock where we could rest without removing packs, catch our breath, and talk it over. Lucky thing Dick hadn't been portaging the canoe; there was no way he could have given me a hand. I was especially lucky he'd had strength enough for us both!

Some strength of my own was returning; a second wind. We decided to keep going together, no matter how far the lake was. From that point on the portage began a slow descent, gradually improving. Then, at last, the long awaited moment—a bend in the trail and a sparkle of azure filtering through green leaves. Nothing in my life had ever looked so good!

It was late in the afternoon when we finally had the canoe and all our gear transported across the backbreaking portage and were ready to shove off. Altogether it had taken more than two hours. Dick pushed the canoe out from the muddy landing, then hesitated, frowning at the expanse of water extending to the right. To the left was a dead end inlet.

"Something's wrong. The lake should be in the other direction," he said darkly.

I was too tired to care—it was a lake and that was good enough for me. We climbed in, paddling unevenly toward open water. Dick glowered at the map in silence, dipping his paddle in occasionally; I struggled to keep on course. Rounding a point, we came upon two men in a canoe fishing near shore. People! Nothing can equal solitude in the wilderness unless it's finding people when you need them. We called out as soon as we were within earshot.

They looked up in surprise. "Swamp Lake," one of them answered Dick's question.

We stared at each other. How could it be? Steering in close enough to talk, we held the canoe still with our paddles.

No, they had never heard of the small lake—hadn't known a portage existed where we'd come from. They seemed to find our story just short of incredible; but obviously we'd had a rough afternoon. If we were looking for a campsite there was one on the other side of the lift-over into Sag, one of them said, pointing across the bay.

We thanked them and set off, finding the portage an easy matter of rolling the canoe across logs. Luck was with us; the campsite was on a high breezy point of land and unoccupied. Added bonus: a sheltered cove behind the point for private bathing!

Tired but refreshed after a cooling swim and freeze dried spaghetti and meatball supper, we spread the map out on the picnic table. Instead of going due east as the portage showed, we had trekked north to the western tip of Swamp Lake, thereby completely bypassing the small lake we were supposed to cross. The portage shown on the map simply didn't exist. An outfitter well acquainted with the BWCA later affirmed this. What we had discovered was an old overgrown winter trail, never used in summer because of the swamps. (Well, almost never!)

As soon as we got hold of a geological survey map we found the winter trail marked with all its twists and bends across the swamps, adding up to about a half mile in all. (The portage shown on the other map would have crossed an impossible hundred-foot ridge!) Altogether we had hiked a mile and a half of swamps interspersed with sharp rises that long afternoon. "Moose Track Torture Portage," I dubbed it in my diary.

Before we put the map away Dick pointed out our route for the next day. We would start off moving out into the wide open part of Lake Saganaga, round American Point, then head down into Red Rock Bay. About 10 miles of straight paddling; no portaging. Looked like a good day, he said. Any day without a portage had to be better than good, I said.

Chapter 4
Wild Waves

Principal Lakes: Saganaga, Red Rock Bay, Red Rock, Alpine

Surfing in an aluminum canoe is not a sport I've ever heard of, but that's exactly what we were doing down Big Sag the next morning. A west wind at our backs through the lower bays of Saganaga Lake quickly developed gale force as we paddled out into open water. Before we had time to change our minds we were plunging down into troughs and up over the tops of big waves, small whitecaps breaking around us. Dick didn't have to tell me to paddle hard. If we were caught sideways in a trough I could see we'd easily swamp.

By the time we'd gone a half mile the waves were three or four feet high and half again the length of the canoe. I don't remember being frightened. We set a course about a quarter mile from the shoreline; the wind and waves would have washed us ashore had we capsized. It was an exhilerating, exciting ride. The closest I can recall to feeling that way before was astride and in control of a spirited, galloping horse. But that was years ago. Dick told me later that paddling to keep ahead of the wave crests gave him the feeling he'd had watching Hawaiian beach boys on TV maneuvering outrigger surfboats to catch rollers. He had to keep reminding himself this was real!

Passing a small island on our galloping ride, we saw a group of people and a motorboat pulled up on shore. Someone raced to the lake edge and aimed a movie camera, following us as we sped past. The gleaming canoe, paddles stroking fast and my red bandanna flapping in the wind must have provided a colorful subject. We've often wished we could have seen the pictures.

The distance covered in this fashion was about two miles in something less than 20 minutes. We saw no other small craft on the lake. Just before coming to American Point there were eight or ten canoes lined up on shore; young people milling around the campsite stared disconsolately out at the wild waves. No doubt a wind-bound party whose destination was in the opposite direction.

Rounding the wide blunt point, we paddled into an almost dead calm produced by the sheltering shores. It was hard to believe we were in the same body of water. We headed down into Red Rock Bay and were soon travelling in the direction we'd come from. The wind picked up considerably as we entered an open reach. Now we were bucking it, using all our strength with every stroke, until we reached the shelter of small islands. Pulling in on one for lunch, we noticed a campsite on the tip of a large island nearby that appeared to be unoccupied. It was early to stop but this looked too good to pass up.

It was. A picnic table and fire grate were located on a pleasant area under shady trees with plenty of room for a tent. It even had a nice rock beach. Ideal—with one exception. Black flies buzzed everywhere. We couldn't figure it out, until we discovered a path leading to a hollow heaped with cans that must have been collecting for years. Most were old and rusty but still attracting hordes of flies. It was appalling that people would leave such an ugly reminder of their presence. We headed back to the canoe and left as fast as we could.

The year was 1964. Worse conditions existed at many of the non-official campsites where campers had devised their own tables and benches, nailing or tying logs together. Trees were scarred with nails, branches hacked off, and makeshift furniture attached to them. The inevitable pile of cans lay heaped in back hollows or partly concealed under bushes.

In 1966 the Forest Service began a clean-up campaign and the results have been spectacular. They started with a project to remove all nonburnable trash, sending out work crews with large burlap bags. It is a rarity to find even one can on a campsite today and that's probably old and rusty, so well camouflaged it escaped notice. (Unfortunately, in spite of signs, pit toilets still seem to be some campers' idea of garbage disposals.) New regulations were made and strictly enforced, banning all but burnable containers for food, with the exception of reusable plastic ones.

Campsites also underwent change. With the tremendous upswing in the number of campers in the '60s, new sites had to be built. Many former non-official ones were equipped with fire grates set in cement and box toilets located on high ground far back from the lakes. Picnic tables, no longer considered appropriate for wilderness camping, have been gradually removed; no new ones built.

But that day was before the change and we were looking

for the convenience of a table. We would have performed a clean-up job on the fly-infested site—we'd done it before and seen evidence of others having done the same—but the can pile was overwhelming and we hadn't brought along a camp shovel.

Red Rock Bay is divided into two sections by a narrows. By the time we'd paddled into the lower bay we'd passed three or four occupied campsites and found no vacant ones. It was midafternoon; neither of us wanted to portage to the next lake. A tiny island across the bay near shore offered an apron of rock but appeared too densely wooded for a campsite. We stroked over to it anyway and got out to stretch our legs. I was investigating a higher, more level area of the rock when I heard Dick's voice in the brush.

"Want to sleep on an innerspring mattress tonight?" he called out.

"Where in the world are you?" I yelled back, pushing aside bushes and ducking under branches trying to locate him. Suddenly I found myself in a small open glen. It was as though I had happened on a stage bathed in green light—walls and roof leafy yellow-green; a deeper, bluer shade below. I started across to where Dick was standing and sank three or four inches in cloud-soft carpeting. A layer of moss, springy deep and bone dry, covered the whole area.

"Wow—we won't even need air mattresses!" I laughed.

Dick had our bedroom set up in short order, tying tent ropes to low branches and using large rocks to secure the corners (common procedure in this glacial country, the dirt layer often too shallow to drive in pegs). It took longer to construct the kitchen; small rocks had to be gathered to build a fireplace for the small grate we carried with us. Usually every expanse of granite big enough to move around on has a pile of blackened rocks where someone once had a cook fire, but there was no evidence anyone had stopped here before.

The fireplace turned out well. We dined on beef stew and pan biscuits and enjoyed a quiet evening on our front porch rock, watching a pair of loons dive for their supper. What our campsite lacked in size and facilities was more than made up for by its pristine nature and lack of flies.

The sun had dropped behind the horizon and we were thinking about readying things for night when we noticed a canoe rounding the point from the narrows, heading for our campsite. As the distance shortened we saw a large man in the stern seat, wearing a Navy captain's hat, a boy about 13 paddling in the bow,

Dick Stresau in camp at Alpine Lake

and a boy and girl of about 8 and 10 sitting forlornly among the packs.

"Could you please tell us where the portage to Red Rock Lake is?" the man called out politely. "We've been going up and down inlets all day."

"Show you on the map," Dick offered, going down to the lake edge to meet him. We invited them all up on shore but the children seemed too weary to move. Their father climbed out, producing a map of the Superior National Forest—on such a small scale the whole BWCA was included! He had never canoed this area before or taken a portage. "Don't know where we are," he said, somehow not sounding the least dismayed.

Dick pointed out on our map the location of the portage, which luckily wasn't far. Once oriented, it didn't take our visitor long to figure out the route. He climbed back into the canoe, thanking us profusely, and paddled off, the children calling thanks too. By now dusk was settling fast. We wondered how they were going to find a campsite in the dark—let alone pitch a tent. But in spite of his problems the captain seemed calm and capable. "Captain and the Kids," we dubbed them after the once popular comic strip.

Our moss mattress was most comfortable but we did not spend a restful night. Our little island must have been the favorite swim-in restaurant of neighborhood beavers. Time and again we were shocked awake by the slap of a broad tail smacking water close by. (We could figure no other explanation for the sound.) We'd lie awake awhile hearing noisy snacking on the willow branches edging our shore; then another sharp crack as a hefty rodent dove off the rocks—probably carrying back "takeouts" to stock his pantry. Whatever they were doing they were "busy as beavers" all night long.

We awoke to sunshine, birdsong and the promise of a good travelling day. "Let's see how fast we can get off," Dick said.

"How about beef stew for breakfast then?" I suggested. "So we won't have to figure out a way to carry it."

Somehow both of us found it a great idea. I wrote in my diary: "Such a breakfast at home would have turned me green but here it seemed just right. I don't know why—eating habits and needs are different on camping trips."

It took exactly an hour from getting up to shoving off— good time even for experts, I'd read somewhere. For us it was breaking all records. It was now the eighth day of our trip. We could have made it back but decided to enjoy the remaining two days with a stopover on Alpine, the last lake before completing the circle to Seagull.

Instead of unloading for the short portage into Red Rock Lake we found we could squirm through a small stream. Stroking leisurely, we came upon a nice campsite about halfway down the lake and there, comfortably settled in, were The Captain and the Kids. The children were splashing and swimming, having a great time, while the captain sat on a rock smoking his pipe, watching. He waved and called out as we went by, thanking us again for our help. We felt greatly cheered and relieved to find things going so well for them all.

In a couple of hours we had paddled the length of the lake and portaged an easy 48 rods into Alpine. Coming out of a narrow inlet, we glanced up at cliffs rising about 40 feet above us on the right. Ahead a sapphire bay sparkled in the sunlight. As we moved out into it, I glanced back and my paddle stopped midair. On this side of the cliffs, nestled on a rocky ledge about halfway down, was the most inviting campsite I'd ever seen; it even had a sheltered sloping rock beach in front. And not a soul in sight!

Even though early in the day, we decided to take advantage and swung the canoe around. The campsite turned out to be remarkable in more ways than one. For the first (and only) time we found platforms for tents, benches and shelves built between trees. All were made out of about two-inch-diameter logs, tied firmly together with thin nylon cord; no nails. It was a good construction job, neatly done, and must have taken hours—probably a camp counselor's idea of a group project, we surmised. Dick set up the tent on one of the platforms and I made use of the handy shelves for pots, pans and small articles. Although an official campsite, it lacked a picnic table. We were most appreciative.

When describing these log constructions to a couple of rangers later, we met with a different attitude. To them it meant a job of tearing it all apart. Such things destroy the wilderness character of campsites, they explained. It was the beginning of stricter regulations in the BWCA. We could only agree they made sense.

But that morning we hadn't come to seeing things in that light. We set up camp, happily making use of the conveniences, then spent a relaxed day swimming, sunbathing and exploring nearby bays and inlets. Supper was freeze dried creamed chicken over yesterday's biscuits and a caramel pudding experiment. I had bought the package at the outfitter's with misgivings. But with water added as directed and beaten with a fork, it thickened as indicated and tasted wonderful.

We were sitting on rocks high above the lake that evening, admiring pink-purplish clouds and their reflections in the calm water below when we heard loons. Their eerie cries started on a low note, rising in a fast glissando to three or four seconds of high pitched yodeling. Then an answering call, sometimes far off. The air was soon filled with their calls. We couldn't see the birds but the sounds seemed to be coming from beyond a point of land just out of view. Intrigued, we put the canoe in the water and paddled over to investigate.

On the other side of the point we discovered five or six loons in a wide open bay. Letting the canoe drift to a stop on the glassy surface, we sat very still. The birds were cavorting haphazardly, it seemed to us, making excited noises, stretching up to flap wings. Now and then one would emit a wavering call, attracting airborne loons flying arrow-straight for the bay. One by one they came down for landings, skidding over the surface some distance like sea planes, before coming to a stop. Soon their numbers had increased to a dozen or more circling closely, their cries becoming shorter, more staccato—all the earmarks of a convention, committee members expressing heated opinions!

By some unseen signal the meeting suddenly broke up with a foot race. Two or more, in some cases four or five, formed a line and began running across the water in an upright position, short wings flailing, at an incredible speed for a quarter of a mile or so until finally airborne. Sometimes they turned back to try again before their heavy bodies lifted from the water. Except for the sound of rhythmically beating wings as they flew overhead, they were silent now as they headed for distant lakes. Perhaps to dine at a favorite fishing spot agreed upon at the conference?

In our reading about loons we have learned that they are considered among the world's finest diving birds, known to go as deep as 80 feet in some instances. They can stay under water as long as eight minutes, reappearing in a spot far distant from where they dived. On land, however, they move clumsily with legs set far back; they can take to the air only from water. Recently Dick and I read an article by a naturalist who discovered that the trilling sounds are made by beakfuls of water gargled and sprayed out with each call. His unique photographs seemed to verify this.

Not much is known about the total loon population but the encroachment of man is threatening breeding grounds and driving the birds farther north to remote areas. We can only hope the wild, eerie cry of the loon will remain a prominent part of the BWCA wilderness.

Dick was studying the map when I came back from rinsing the breakfast dishes the next morning.

"Bet we can get into Seagull without portaging," he said, showing me a long arm extending northeast from Alpine and bending around to connect with Seagull. "Could be rapids at that narrow point," he added.

"Let's go see—then we'll know ahead," I said.

He agreed, suggesting we pack a lunch. Looked like a good day to be out on the lakes, our last before starting back in the morning.

The long, crooked arm extended about a mile, easily navigable until we approached the narrow place where the water grew increasingly shallow and fast; we could hear rapids around a bend. Dick steered the canoe in to shore and hiked across the brush to take a look. "Don't think we better try getting a loaded canoe through," he said on his return. "Too shallow and lots of rocks."

I breathed a secret sigh of relief. The mere thought of shooting rapids had scared up some butterflies but I didn't want to admit it. The rest of the day we spent exploring the lower end of Alpine, hiking a trail to Rog Lake where we ate lunch on a shady rock near the water. A pair of panhandling jays showed up to entertain and share the goodies.

When we returned to our campsite westerly breezes had

shifted to a stiff southeast wind. As we set about preparing supper, enjoying our airy quarters, we noticed an uncommonly large number of canoeists coming out of the portage inlet, having hard work paddling into the wind. Invariably they glanced up with unhappy expressions as they passed our campsite and saw it occupied. Two young women in particular made us wish later we'd called them back, at least for a rest and bite to eat. They were in separate canoes with a child in the bow of each, despair written on tired faces as they struggled to make headway. (The next morning we passed them emerging from thick shoreline brush on an island, wearily lugging gear to canoes pulled up on rocks. It must have been a dreadful night.)

A few canoeists called up to inquire about campsites but we could give little help. It was hard to believe all the people, while two days ago we'd seen no one at all for 48 hours. The answer, of course, lay in the routes—or, more correctly, the portages. Alpine Lake was part of a well travelled loop from Big Sag to Seagull, relatively short with easy portages. If you were willing to tackle longer routes with portages like those into Ester, you could undoubtedly enjoy any number of lakes to yourself. We haven't been back to the Alpine-Seagull area recently but have learned that the Forest Service has constructed several new campsites. In the last year or two reservations have been required which helps alleviate the problem of overcrowding in popular areas.

Instead of dropping at sundown, the wind grew to gale force. All night long the tent billowed noisily, flaps pulling loose and slapping against the nylon sides, waves crashing on the rocks below. Sleep was sketchy. In the morning heavy clouds blocked the sun but, at least, no rain. We decided to pack up and get off before the weather got worse. Loading the canoe was tricky with high waves pounding it sideways against the rocks; impossible to hold it off. We worked fast. The packs in, Dick grabbed a paddle and jumped into the stern seat. No time to think. I planted a foot solidly up in the front, grasped the gunwales with both hands, and gave a mighty push with the other foot. To my amazement—I'd been fully prepared to end up in the lake—the bow swung neatly off the rocks, I landed in the bow seat, and we were off, stroking hard into the teeth of the gale.

"Nice going!" Dick sang out from the rear.

I basked in his approval, mighty pleased with myself. It was a tough fight against the wind but we were working together like a team now, confidence oozing out of every pore—at least mine. I could have tackled a tidal wave! Whenever I get cocky I should know I'm in for a lesson but I'm always caught unaware. I had a day to wait this time.

After a strenuous mile of paddling we reached the shelter of islands; the rest of the way was easy. By the time we had the gear transported over the portage and were ready to shove off into Seagull, clouds were thinning and it looked like the sun might soon be out. Across a short bay we noticed an unoccupied campsite— easy to find early in the day. Its long reach of rocks made a wonderful beach.

"Let's stay!" I said impulsively.

Dick's eyebrows shot up. "You mean it?"

"Why not? We've got enough food for one more day."

He was more than willing to prolong the trip but a little surprised. I was too, to tell the truth. I really hadn't known how much I didn't want it to end. Almost all our canoe trips have been the same since then. They may sometimes get off to bad starts but I never want to go home.

It was a jimdandy campsite. We even found a massive flat rock coffee table with rock seats pushed near on an open ledge convenient to the cook fire. By afternoon the sun was shining in a cloudless sky and we set off toward cliffs across a wide bay to the east, the same bay we'd be crossing in the morning. As usual Dick had blueberries as well as cliff climbing in mind. However, he'd hardly gone a few yards when he came hurrying back, arms waving around his head. Yellowjackets had testily disputed his right to trespass, stinging him four or five times. A couple had even gotten under his shirt, luckily not on his face. I always carry a few first aid items wherever we go, so we rubbed a little salve on the angry red welts. Dick's spirit of adventure considerably diminished, we headed back. A soda and water paste helped relieve the swelling and pain once we got in camp.

In the morning he was fine. But not the weather. It had rained a little in the night and a cold damp wind was blowing from the north, threatening more rain. We broke camp and set off about 9 a.m. This time the wind was coming across the bay at an angle from the stern. It didn't look too bad from shore but proved difficult out on the lake. Yesterday I'd been sure we could handle anything, but neither of us was prepared for the growing size of the waves as the wind's distance over the water increased. By the time we were halfway across, the choppy waves were only an inch or two short of coming over the gunwales at the canoe's midsection. Fortunately I was much too busy to glance back and Dick made sure I remained uninformed until later.

I could see the cresting waves foaming around us and paddled hard to keep the canoe from slipping sideways in the troughs. Each time we plunged down into a hollow and started up the other side I leaned back as far as I could, hoping to lighten the bow so it could rise over the crests. They came so close to breaking over it I felt spray on my face but we didn't ship water.

The wild ride ended when we paddled safely into the protection of Three Mile Island, which we could follow on the lee side almost to our takeoff point on Seagull. The map showed about a quarter mile of open water between the end of the island and the inlet; not wide enough to be a problem, we thought. With three miles to travel in the shelter of the big island it was wonderful to relax tired muscles, paddle slowly and chat. "Maybe the wind will have dropped by the time we get to the open place," Dick remarked. "We can handle big waves anyway," I gloated— "nothing to worry about.". . . The time was ripe. As I said, I'm always caught unaware.

Coming out of the lee of the island, we paddled left around a point and immediately found out that rather than dropping the wind had increased! The open stretch was a seething mass of whitecapped, dark purple waves, bigger than any I'd ever seen on the lakes. What we had neglected to notice on the map was a long reach of unprotected water the wind would be blowing down across. The waves had been whipped to tremendous size. There was no way to reach Seagull boat landing except by crossing them; we had no choice.

Dick steered out into the wind. We paddled furiously to take the oncoming waves head-on, climbing up over each crest to be thrust helplessly sideways down into the next trough. More furious paddling to swing the canoe once again in a position to rise up over the top of the next wave. Meeting it side-on would have meant swamping. I glanced at the shoreline once and we seemed to be slipping backwards. It was taking every ounce of my strength as it was; we'd never make it. Thoroughly frightened, I yelled at Dick to turn back to the island. But of course we couldn't. Turning around in this sea would have spelled disaster.

All I could do was keep pitting my strength against the fury of the wind and water. More than once a super-sized wave broke over the bow, soaking me to the skin, water sweeping into the canoe. But by then Dick and I were working together in rhythm, each upholding the other's strokes by our own maneuvers. I knew that we'd make it.

When we finally reached the other side I begged to pull in to shore to rest before hunting for the inlet. Dick kept paddling, arguing that it was just the other side of the point we were approaching. To my amazement he was right. As soon as we entered the narrow neck it was as though somebody had turned off the wind. The finish of the trip was made in calm waters.

Within an hour the packs were transferred to the car, the canoe was tied on top, and we were heading back for the civilized world. Not without reluctance but at least with the satisfaction of having had a great time and a memorable trip. My cocksureness about handling wild waves had been knocked down several pegs but we hadn't swamped or capsized and I had learned something. That I was to be back in a few weeks learning more would never have occurred to me. At least next time it would be someone else's lesson.

Chapter 5
Nor'Westers on the Big Lakes

Principal Lakes: Seagull, Brule, North and South Temperance

It was probably the excitement on our 10-year-old Steve's face that inspired our return to Seagull Lake that summer. Camp had been okay but the account of our canoe adventures had him on the edge of his chair. How soon could he go with us, he wanted to know—ready to dash out the door that minute.

Dick and I exchanged glances. He had taken all the vacation he should but perhaps a long weekend the end of August, enough to give Steve a taste of camping. It didn't take long to decide. We were as eager as he and admittedly glad for an excuse to go back.

Late summer in northern Minnesota is unpredictable. I stuffed heavy shirts, extra socks and raincoats into the clothing pack, feeling foolish. The temperature had been in the nineties the last two days and there wasn't a cloud in the sky that morning.

We shoved off from Seagull Lake boat landing early Saturday afternoon. Our destination was a campsite at the end of the lake, across the bay from where we'd last camped. It was on a jutting peninsula called Shirttail Point (for reasons we've never learned). On our previous trip we had remarked about the picturesque cliffs towering above the campsite.

Luck was with us; it was unoccupied. Having been scrunched in among the gear most of the 5-mile-long paddle, Steve leaped out on shore with an excited whoop and headed for a path leading up the bluff. As soon as we'd set up camp we joined him. Even I enjoyed these cliffs, flat and grassy on top with a spectacular view of the big, sprawling lake, and a trail that wound instead of going straight up. We all brought back armloads of deadwood for the supper fire. I don't recall what we cooked but I do know we ate heartily.

In the evening we paddled out onto a mirror-calm bay, Steve and I taking turns in the bow. The sun set in a haze, bathing the shoreline in a rosy glow. We snapped pictures of Steve proudly manning the canoe alone in our sheltered cove. There was no danger; the air hung heavy and still. As soon as it began to grow dark we turned in. Steve was too excited to sleep. We lay awake listening to loons calling and, far away, the repeated eerie cries of a screech owl.

I don't know how much later I was awakened by howling wind and rain lashing the tent. Dick and I struggled out of sleeping bags to tie shut the billowing tent flaps. We tried to go back to sleep but the storm grew in intensity. Not having considered the possibility of a storm, we had foolishly pitched the tent on a narrow strip of land between cliffs and rocks, facing directly into the gale without even trees for protection.

Rain kept blowing in under the flaps, soaking the front end of the tent. We covered the sleeping bags with a tarp and pulled the mattresses back as far as possible. Except for a few sleepy mutterings Steve, nestled in his bag between us, slept soundly through it all. Short naps were the best we could manage the rest of the night.

In the morning the nor'wester continued unabated. Whitecapped waves, whipped to a frenzy in the gale winds, crashed on the rocky shore, sending up great plumes of white spray. We were glad we didn't plan to return today; it was no weather to be out in a small boat. But on shore it was exciting. Donning extra clothes and raincoats (thank goodness I'd brought them!), we ran to the shore for a close-up view of the raging elements, our faces wet with rain and spray.

The fire grate and picnic table were located at the other end of the campsite, protected from the wind by a thick stand of spruce. Having learned our lesson on Ester Lake, we had dry firewood with which to start the breakfast fire; pancakes and steaming cups of coffee (cocoa for Steve) weren't long in coming. Dick strung a tarp above the table and we ate in relatively dry comfort. He considered moving the tent but decided everything would get wetter in the process. After breakfast we shoved the mattresses away from the door, piled the sleeping bags to make comfortable backrests, and played an old family favorite guessing game, "animal, vegetable or mineral?" Now and then we'd venture outside to stretch cramped legs and dash to the rocks to marvel at the size of the waves, some shooting spray 10 feet in the air when they broke.

Steve's bright yellow slicker struck a gay note in the gray world as he ran and leaped about. Once we spied a power boat far out on the bay, making slow progress as it dipped and rose with the waves. Until late afternoon it was the only boat we saw.

Instead of letting up as the day wore on, the wind increased and the rain came down harder than ever. Dick was trying to get a fire started and I was beginning supper preparations when Steve came running from the shore. "Canoes are coming!" he shouted excitedly.

I'm not sure if either of us really believed him but we should have. At the lake edge he pointed to two canoes a good distance out in the bay, heading in our direction. We could barely make out the dark figures bent over paddles. Foam-topped waves appeared to be outracing them, washing over their sterns. We ran out on the rocks for a better view, wondering how we could help. As they came closer we saw there were five men in hooded ponchos, two in the lead boat, three in the other. Finally the first canoe lurched into our cove, crash-landing on the rocks, so full of water there was no other way. Swung broadside by the force of the waves, it almost turned over with each breaker.

Dick raced to grab hold and steady the boat while the men climbed out. Then all three struggled to pull the water-laden craft up on shore. The second canoe, riding even lower in the water with its heavier crew, scraped bottom farther out. The men stepped over the side into the surf, striving to keep their balance on the slippery rocks. When all were on shore the canoes were dragged up as far as possible. Their sodden packs were removed and the boats turned over. Gallons of water poured from each. For a few minutes all of us stood around exclaiming.

"You sure had us worried," I remarked.

"You worried!" one of the older men said, shaking his head. "Another hundred feet and we'd have swamped!"

"We couldn't see the shore it was raining so darned hard," another commented. "Don't know how we'd have made it without this young fella's bright yellow raincoat." He smiled down at Steve. "Kept aiming for that."

The unwitting hero of the day grinned from ear to ear, thoroughly enjoying his importance.

The men were anxious to check their map with ours. In spite of the near disaster they wanted to go on if they could. We took shelter under trees and Dick pointed out Three Mile Island, just the other side of our campsite. Paddling in its lee would give shelter most of the way, except for the short open stretch where we had run into big waves before.

They decided to chance it. The two younger members of their party were college students due back for classes day after next, with a long drive to Chicago in the offing. They had started out from their camp on a small lake this morning, they said, intending to get back today. It was raining hard and blowing, but they hadn't run into any trouble until they'd paddled out onto Seagull too far to turn back without danger of swamping or capsizing. They'd had no idea of the size of waves storm winds can whip up on a big lake. It was a lesson for all of us.

The nor'wester blew itself out sometime during the night, as unexpectedly as it had started. We awoke to a quiet, sunny morning. Steve and his father tried a little cliff climbing across a nearby inlet and then we paddled over to hike the portage to Alpine Lake, breaking camp and starting for home after lunch. In spite of the storm it had been a fine weekend—complete with excitement, drama, and a happy ending. We now had another eager canoe camper in the family. Three in a pack-laden canoe, even an 18 footer, is not the best way to travel, however. It was a problem we were to solve the following summer in a way that enriched all our lives in the years to come. We added Mike.

Steve and Mike Randall had been buddies since second grade. As we lived on a lake 10 miles out in the country and the Randalls in town, the boys often spent weekends at one another's houses. It seemed a good idea to include Mike on our next trip, letting the two try manning their own canoe. Having spent much of their lives on or around Wisconsin lakes, both boys were good swimmers and familiar with small boats. The Randalls were not only enthusiastic and appreciative of our taking Mike but offered to return the favor by keeping Steve while Dick and I took a canoe trip alone later. It was an arrangement we were to follow and benefit from until the boys reached 16 and were taking their own trips.

As I look back on it now, I wonder that Steve and Mike's first canoe trip the following June didn't discourage them forever. It got off to a bad start with a two hour wait in the car at the boat landing due to an unrelenting downpour. On the portages tiny black biting flies drove us crazy, clustering on any exposed skin, even sneaking under pant cuffs and shirttails. Bug spray did little good. (We have since learned that the only way to beat these pests is to stay home during June!) Toughest of all for the inexperienced young paddlers was the distance covered before we could locate a vacant campsite. We finally settled for a grassy open place on top of a steep banking.

A hearty stew and biscuits did much to revive tired muscles and flagging spirits but the chocolate pudding treat I'd brought along turned out to be pure disaster. Somehow I read the directions wrong and doubled the quantity of water! (My liquid dessert became a joke the boys never allowed me to forget—especially when on a future trip they made a chocolate pudding that turned out perfectly!)

After supper the two had fun choosing a level secluded spot and setting up their tent, but during the night it poured again and turned cold. They were still asleep when we got up but soon appeared, glum faced and shivering. Their tent had leaked, soaking the bottom ends of their sleeping bags and some of their clothes. Apparently they had slept too soundly to notice until morning. We set them to work at once, gathering and chopping firewood to get circulation going. By the time they had worked awhile and drunk steaming cups of cocoa around the fire, they were warm and cheerful again, eager to start the day's adventures.

Rain was still threatening, however. Dick and I talked it over and came to the conclusion it was wiser to leave rather than take a chance on another wet night. Our decision met with howls of protest. It did seem mean to abort the trip they had looked forward to for so long.

"Tell you what, guys," Dick said. "We'll take you on another trip in August—with your own pup tent. You can try it out in the backyard first." (We had rented their tent and canoe.)

When they were convinced this was a bona fide promise, faces brightened once more.

Paddling came a little easier for the boys on the trip back, with less zigging and zagging; the cold had taken care of most of the blackflies; and by the time we were driving home the happy babble in the back seat left no doubt that Steve and Mike had joined the ranks of enthusiastic canoe trippers.

Before making good on our promise to the boys in August, Dick and I were to experience our second nor'wester. This time it was on Brule, a king-sized lake with interesting bays and portages to smaller lakes. We set forth in July to explore this new area alone. The map showed an unpaved access road to Brule Lake but gave no indication of the condition. It took us two hours to travel its 5-mile length, crawling in, out and over potholes and rocks. (The road has since been rebuilt with a good gravel surface.) Deep ruts and dense waist-high brush on both sides made it impossible to circumvent most of the obstacles in the narrow, one-track road.

Scraping bottom more than once, our Pontiac finally came to a complete halt about halfway through. Back wheels spun in holes while her undersides remained securely jammed on grass and rocks. We got out to search for something to lever up the back end but found nothing. Ten or 15 minutes later a car labored around the bend and came to a stop behind us. Two men got out to help, there being no way to get past. Efforts to lift and shove got nowhere. By then a car was approaching from the opposite direction. How we'd all get out of this wilderness traffic jam, I couldn't imagine!

Luckily the third car was a four-wheel-drive vehicle, able to pull up over the ruts and park in the thick brush. Three burly men climbed out, exchanging lighthearted banter as they scrutinized the situation. Nothing to worry about—they'd have her rolling in no time, they claimed. They were right. With the combined strength of all six men the car was raised enough to shove her free.

We thanked them all and were on our painstaking way again, luckily needing no further assistance. With considerable relief we finally topped a rise to find Brule's sapphire bay sparkling below. Near the end of the trail was a campground with two or three tents and some cars parked nearby. We wondered if the campers had known about the road and considered the lake worth the trip, or had found out on the way in as we did.

When we pulled up to the boat dock a young couple was loading their canoe, a stack of gear piled messily on the pier. I was surprised to see plastic bags instead of packs. When I caught sight of a Coleman stove among the stuff I labeled them the greenest of greenhorns. They'd learn a thing or two on the portages, I smiled to myself. This being our fifth canoe trip, we'd show the folks gathered on the dock the difference between amateurs and professionals! (True to form I was wading straight into a lesson, completely unaware.)

Dick tied the canoe to the side of the pier and we began briskly stacking our canvas packs in a neat row along the edge. This year we had replaced the cardboard food box with a trim pack basket. Curved to fit the back, with wide carrying straps, it was comfortable and easy to portage (at least after a day or two of eating!). I was about to hand our fine new addition over to Dick for loading when I noticed something thick and brown seeping through the slats, running down one side. A whiff told me. Peanut butter! Grabbing tissues, I hastily wiped the basket, then unbuckled its canvas cover to tighten the lid on the plastic peanut butter container.

The horror scene that met my eyes will live with me forever! Bumps and jolts over the rough road had either unscrewed or knocked off the top. Peanut butter had spilled down in thick rivers, coating everything it touched like wet cement!

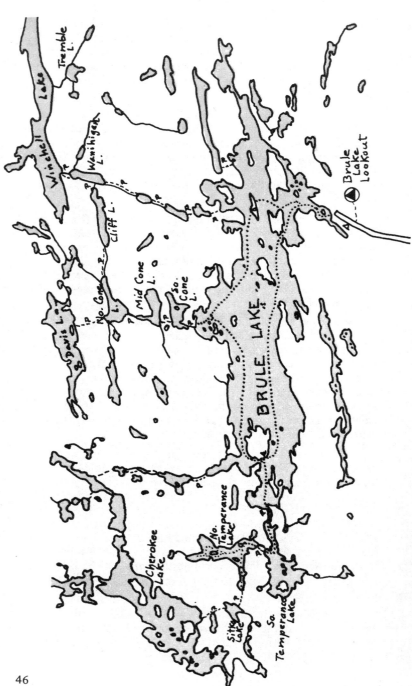

Impatient at the delay, Dick strode over to see what the trouble was. One look and he slung the basket to his shoulder and transported it over near a trash can by the dock.

"Get towels—we'll have to unpack and clean it up piece by piece," he called.

Walking past the campers, I tried to smile as though peanut butter running amuck in one's food basket was an amusing annoyance. I was met only with stares tinged with contempt. It was very clear who had won the greenhorn award!

About a half hour later a good portion of the spill had been scraped back into the container, the lid tightly fastened, and everything cleaned and repacked. Dick loaded the basket among the packs and we were off. Our audience had long since lost interest and vanished.

Heading west out of the bay, we passed islands of all sizes, some with inviting campsites, none occupied. Our destination was the far end of the lake where a 6-rod portage would take us into South Temperance Lake, our planned stop for the night.

As we slowly made our way down the vast reach of Brule, I felt a growing sense of magnificent wildness. There was no sign of a boat or of humanity anywhere the whole afternoon. A stiff breeze was blowing from the southwest, stirring up a choppy sea. After four or more miles my arms were crying for a rest. It was close to five o'clock and both of us were getting hungry, having eaten only a snack lunch in the car before turning onto the Brule road. We were approaching a large island. "If there's a campsite, let's stop," I suggested. Dick agreed but there was no sign of a break in the shoreline brush as we stroked past. Once again my habit of glancing back paid off. Beneath tall trees at an angle that couldn't have been seen from the side was an opening. Dick swung the canoe around.

It was indeed a campsite, an excellent one, almost out of sight beneath towering Norway pines. A thick layer of russet-brown needles provided attractive wall-to-wall carpeting for the extensive kitchen-dining-bedroom area; a Forest Service fire grate stood ready with storage table nearby; and "facilities" were located down a path in the back. What a delightful ending to a day of delays and frustrations!

It was a starlit night when we turned in but we awoke to cold, dense fog and intermittent bursts of rain. Unless there's a need to travel, rainy days are reading days for us; we had brought along books. Most of the morning we spent reading in the tent, burrowed warmly into sleeping bags. After a lunch of bone-warming bean soup, hot tea, fruit and cookies, we set off to explore a deep inlet at our end of the lake. The rain had stopped and after awhile the sun came out. We hiked the portage we found at the end, slippery rocks, mud and swarms of mosquitoes making us glad we wouldn't be coming this way in the morning.

A depressing fog settled in again after supper; with only three days left we would go on the next day whatever the conditions. The fog was still with us when we awoke but it had become very warm and humid. Everything we touched was wet; even the inside walls and floor of the tent. It was uncomfortable, uninspiring weather. We moved sluggishly breaking camp.

I was dipping a bucketful of water from the still lake for dishwashing when I noticed the young couple we'd seen at the boat dock gliding past in the mist. I waved and they paddled over to chat a while, surprised to see us.

"We thought you must be up in North Temperance Lake by now the way you were getting off to such a fast start," the girl said.

(They hadn't stayed around to witness our peanut butter fiasco.) We grinned sheepishly and I related the ignominious turn of events after their departure. The ice was broken. They in turn recounted some of their less fortunate experiences.

"One trip it was raining so hard it took till noon to get a fire going for a cup of coffee!" the man confided. "I've carried a stove ever since. Believe me, it's worth the extra weight!"

We found out they had camped on South Temperance Lake and had to return tomorrow. Conversation never gets very far in lake country without the inevitable, "How's the fishing?" or "How're they biting?" There's no way to reply except that we haven't been fishing, which always produces puzzled expressions. The simple truth is that while we enjoy eating fish, neither of us likes catching them.

They recovered from their surprise at our admission by telling about the walleye they'd caught for supper last night.

"Great tasting fish—even without salt," the man said pointedly, glancing at his wife. She winced. "I always forget something," she laughed. "This time it was salt."

Before they left I gave them some in a sandwich baggie, for which they were very grateful. Small items take on great importance in the wilderness when there's no corner grocery to which to run.

It was eleven before we finally shoved off. We stopped

for lunch at a campsite on South Temperance Lake and then carried our gear over the 53 rods into North Temperance, easy portaging except for heat, humidity and bugs. The sun had come out blazing hot. Across from the landing we saw a picnic table on a small island with no sign of people and paddled eagerly toward it.

As soon as the tent was pitched under small pines on a knoll, we donned swimsuits and dove into the lake. After the first shock the water was perfect; we stayed in a long time. In the late afternoon, relaxing on air mattresses pulled into the shade under trees, we became aware of the sound of an outboard motor growing louder. We sat up to see a couple of rangers pulling in to our island. "Just checking camping permits," they explained. We showed them ours and chatted awhile, inquiring about the condition of the two portages into Cherokee Lake we had hoped to reach. The first would give us no trouble, they said, but the second, much longer, had some bad climbs. Together the portaging came out to 243 rods with a small pond to get across in between.

We decided to leave Cherokee for another trip and explore the north arm of North Temperance tomorrow, starting back the next day. We'd stop overnight on one of the Cones, a series of small lakes just north of Brule, about halfway down its length.

The following day dawned sunny and hot again. We spent most of it in or on the lake. In the night the wind shifted and we awoke to a brisk northwest breeze with a temperature drop of at least 30 degrees. We broke camp swiftly (for us) and retraced our route, stopping for lunch at the campsite on Brule where we had first stayed. Soon on our way again, we coasted down the lake with a strong following wind. The portage into the first of the Cone lakes started in a marsh under a few inches of water. Pulling off shoes and socks and rolling up pant legs, Dick ventured in for a short distance but it didn't appear to get better. We changed plans and headed back to Brule, deciding to continue until we reached one of the island campsites we'd seen at the start of our trip.

Once out in the wide reach of the big lake, we found ourselves being propelled rapidly forward by winds that had risen to gale force. At this point the waves had travelled so far that they had become long rollers with foaming whitecaps. The farther we went the bigger they got. I searched the near shoreline for a break indicating a campsite but found nothing. There seemed no way to escape our speedy, plunging ride—short of swamping! Dick said nothing but I could guess water was coming close to the gunwales.

CANOEING THE BOUNDARY WATERS

Fear was beginning to get the upper hand when I caught sight of a tiny island on our right—too small for a campsite but there was an opening under trees. A port in the storm, at least. I called back to Dick, pointing it out.

"Let's make a try for it!" he shouted over the noise of the wind. I knew then how close we were to swamping!

To reach the island meant turning dangerously sideways to the big waves. Luckily it wasn't far. There were frightening moments when a wave crest broke over the windward side of the bow, threatening to slap us down into the trough, but hard, fast strokes pushed us up on top again. I was trembling with fatigue and relief when we finally made a jolting landing on the solid rock "beach" of our little haven.

There was a pile of blackened rocks on a jutting bare arm of the island where campfires had been built. It seemed a good idea to make supper there and push off across the bay in the evening when the wind dropped.

By seven o'clock the wind had risen instead and the waves were bigger than ever. A howling nor'wester in full swing! We searched out an open spot under three or four tall pines near the center of the narrow island. Although close to the water on both sides, it was pretty well protected from the north by a thicket of bushes and stunted birches. Dick set up the tent and we crawled in not long after sundown, planning a before-breakfast takeoff when the winds would be calmest.

Inside the tent we felt snug and safe as we listened to the winds and seas boiling around us. I took time to note in the journal our appreciation for this welcome shelter. We had become very fond of our "tight little island."

Sometime after midnight we found out it wasn't as "tight" as we'd thought. We awoke first to the thrashing of the pines above us. Suddenly the tent began billowing in and out like a thing gone mad. Lightning flashed and thunder rolled, followed by a hard downpour that caved in the sides, soaking clothes and everything they contacted. While we were scrambling to move packs and gear to the center, a corner tent peg pulled out, causing the floor to rise up and the ceiling sag to meet it on that side.

Dick grabbed his raincoat and plunged out into the maelstrom. As soon as he secured that peg another blew loose. Finally he weighted down each corner with heavy rocks, found by the illumination of almost constant lightning. When he crawled back inside several minutes later he was as soaked to the skin as though he'd worn no raincoat.

As suddenly as it had started the storm stopped. There was dead calm. I was beginning to relax in the uneasy silence, grateful that the tent hadn't blown down, when it started all over again from the opposite direction—thrashing trees, billowing walls, thunder and lightning, and a deluge. The tent shook and strained at its ropes but the rocks held. In half an hour it had all died away. The rest of the night we slept peacefully.

Awakening with the sun around 6:30, we broke camp as quickly as possible. The wind was still from the northwest and by the time we shoved off it was beginning to pick up real strength again, producing long swells. I was apprehensive about the half mile of open bay to cross but it turned out nothing more than an up and down merry-go-round ride. We soon glided into island-sheltered waters and stopped at a campsite to cook a delicious hot breakfast, both of us hungry as bears by then.

Discussing the experiences of the night, we came to the conclusion that a tornadic storm had hit our small island. Had it been a full-fledged tornado, undoubtedly we would have ended up in the lake. Tent and all!

One thing for sure—we wouldn't chance nor'westers on the big lakes with Steve and Mike next month. Dick had ideas for a trip from West Bearskin to Duncan, moderate-sized lakes near the boundary chain. Out of the far end of Duncan was the historic Staircase Portage that dropped 140 feet to Rose Lake and Canadian waters. We'd camp on Duncan a couple of nights with the boys and paddle over for a look.

Chapter 6
Stairway to the Past

Principal Lakes: Duncan, Rose

From a cliff 140 feet above Rose Lake we gazed across at Canada's forested hills. In the distance Arrow Lake's jutting escarpment added a pink-tinged swath to the greens and blues. Above us towered white pines of at least 200 years' growth while clumps of spruce and balsam fir, edging the flat open area on which we stood, framed the spectacular view. That this impressive overlook was also a campsite, unoccupied, to claim for our own was luck almost beyond belief. As was so often the case with camps labeled "best" (in our personal records), we had come upon it unexpectedly. (Camping no longer is allowed here, but it is still a good lunch stop.)

The night before, beginning our trip with Steve and Mike, we had camped on Duncan Lake. They had been in high spirits, impatient to try out new canoeing skills acquired at Boy Scout camp during the summer, and had even taken turns portaging their 54-pound craft a few yards on the trail from West Bearskin Lake, our starting point. Discovering an open point of land about a mile across from the landing, they were eager to investigate. We followed, admiring their fairly straight course through moderately choppy waves.

Beaching their canoe, they had scrambled up the brushy slope, yelling triumphantly that they'd found a campsite. It would be a good base camp for our three day trip, we all agreed. Everyone got to work setting up camp.

The morning sky was lightly overcast, promising an early burn-off. I packed lunches and we got off by 9 o'clock, heading for the northern finger of Duncan Lake where the famed Staircase Portage descended steeply to Rose Lake. Allowing the boys to stop and explore along the way, we spent a fair part of the morning paddling a couple of miles to the far end of the inlet. Close to noon we pulled our canoes up on marshy ground beside the portage entrance.

The well-beaten trail wound through deep woods beside a shallow, fast running stream. Mike and Steve raced ahead, returning with breathless accounts of a little wooden bridge and a waterfall. We soon came to the bridge, crossing the stream at a right-angled turnoff, and continued on the main path, hearing falls below.

Coniferous trees formed such a thick canopy above that no sunlight penetrated the vaulted ceiling, trapping a damp, piney deep-woods fragrance. We soon came to the first block of steps, which descended to a flat landing with an overlook for viewing the falls. Close to the railing you could feel the spray from the roaring white water, dropping vertically 40 or 50 feet to a deep pool before cascading down over the rocks. We humans looked small and fragile beside this monstrous power; and would certainly be dashed to death on the rocks should we be unlucky enough to get in its way, I thought.

Continuing our descent, we went down a longer block of steps to another flat landing with a place to prop a canoe.

"Shouldn't be hard to get the canoes down," Dick speculated, surveying the well placed rests and broad stairs.

· Each step was constructed of 5- or 6-inch-diameter cedar logs with a solid, dirt-packed backing to provide wide spaces for walking.

Steve and Mike had taken the steps in flying leaps to the bottom and were now coming back up slowly, counting. "Eighty-six steps!" they called when they reached the top.

I wondered what the portage had been like for the Indians and voyageurs before there had been a convenient staircase, which was built by the CCC in the mid-thirties.

Returning to the rustic bridge, we crossed it to investigate a trail beyond and soon emerged at the cliff-top campsite with the breath-taking overlook. We could hardly believe our eyes.

The boys were ecstatic, begging to camp here. Dick pointed out that we had already made our camp and it would be a lot of trouble to move.

"We'll help!" Two pair of earnest blue eyes looked up, shining in their eagerness.

"This campsite's got a waterfall, Daddy!" Steve offered for a crowning argument.

"And a brook—we could wash the dishes in running water!" Mike chimed in to add weight.

We had to agree the attractions were many. But what if

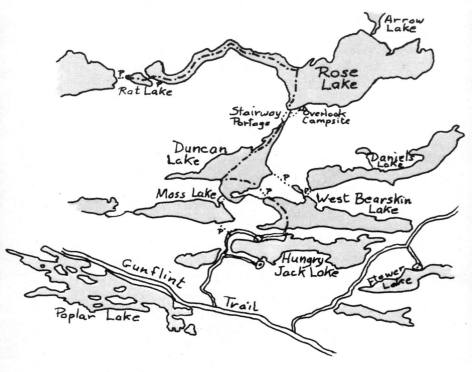

people came in and set up camp here while we were moving? It was a point to consider. In the end we worked out a plan where the boys promised to remain on the campsite with lunches, life belts and other paraphernalia arrayed on the picnic table as "claim stakers" while Dick and I paddled back to pack gear and move camp as fast as possible.

We returned to the waiting boys in something less than two hours to find that all had gone well. Some people had come in to look at the view but no one had wanted to camp. Our exuberant two, having already consumed their lunches, set off to portage packs and assorted gear back from the canoe. While Dick and I were hungrily munching our sandwiches a man with two ladies emerged from the trail. He said he lived in a summer cottage nearby and had brought his visiting cousins to see the view of Canada. He hoped we didn't mind. We assured him we didn't.

During our stay a few others came for the same purpose. It was the first (and only) time we occupied a campsite located on a tourist attraction! As all our visitors were considerate and friendly, we rather enjoyed the chance to chat and exchange view points. One couple in particular we'll never forget.

Dick and the boys met them first when returning from a late afternoon climb up a mountain (Minnesota variety) behind our campsite. The trailless ascent through tangled brush and up sheer rock faces had been difficult but the view at the top well worth it. They had descended by a different route and emerged at the Duncan Lake landing where the man and his wife had just pulled in. Along with the usual camping gear, they were unloading a professional looking movie camera and heavy tripod.

Striking up a conversation, Dick learned that their goal was to film the route the explorer Alexander Mackenzie travelled before 1800—from the Boundary Lakes chain to the Mackenzie River in Canada, and on to the Arctic Ocean. The bearded young man and his attractive wife were professional people, planning to accomplish this ambitious feat in segments during vacations. This was the first. Within two weeks they expected to paddle and portage their equipment 250 miles from Rose Lake to International Falls, filming along the way!

As a lead-off for their documentary they hoped to photograph a panoramic view of the chain lakes from the mountain top, but after talking to Dick the young man decided it would be too difficult and time consuming to tote their camera gear up and back. He readily accepted Dick's invitation to take pictures from our cliff-top overlook.

I was busy tending pots of chicken chowder and stewed dried apples over a too-hot supper fire when the couple arrived so didn't have much time to chat or watch the filming. But they seemed enthusiastic and pleased when they left.

In the morning we saw them once again, this time at the bottom of Staircase Portage. Dick thought it worthwhile to carry both canoes down for a day's excursion to Canadian shores. At the Rose Lake landing the young man had set up his tripod and was filming the lake's eastward expanse with the picturesque Arrow Lake cliffs in the distance. A group of campers coming into the portage had pulled their canoes out on shore and were standing around watching.

"Are you a professional cameraman?" one of them asked.

"No. I'm a biochemist," he replied.

Dick and I exchanged grins, unable to resist the humor. Here was a living version of the popular (at that time) TV cigaret ads! There was always a natural scene background, such as a western ranch, in front of which would be a man in a broad-brimmed hat on horseback smoking. Then someone would ask, "Are you a cowboy?" "No. I'm a physicist," (or something along that line) would come the reply. The only thing missing was the cigaret and background theme song!

The last we saw of the pair was an hour or so later when we were setting off across Rose Lake. Rounding a point ahead to the west the two were leisurely dipping paddles as though they had all day. It was well after 10 o'clock. How they would cover their intended distance, averaging 18 to 20 miles a day (as they must), at that pace we couldn't imagine. We've often wished we knew how the project turned out.

Canada's densely wooded shore, when we reached it, looked the same as the United States' but somehow it was more exciting. We pulled the canoes up on a stony beach and climbed out, feeling adventuresome to be treading on foreign soil. Mike and Steve picked up pebbles for souvenirs and we shoved off again to paddle the length of the long, crooked western arm of Rose Lake. A fairly solid strip of beach at the 4-rod portage into Rat Lake allowed the boys to explore on foot a bit.

"Come see what we found!" a shout soon went up.

They were stooping over something a few feet back from the shore edge, which turned out to be a square bronze plaque set solidly in cement.

"It's a boundary marker put there in the early 1920s by the International Joint Commission," Dick explained. "The commission was set up to establish the boundary after a century of hassling. But there has never been military action—something to be proud of in these times of hot and cold wars between countries."

The four of us crouched over the small historic marker in silence, each lost in his own thoughts.

We didn't explore much farther than Rat Lake that day. The boys were eager for play around the rocks in the campsite stream, where they raced stick boats in the fast current and watched them shoot miniature rapids and waterfalls.

It was late August and, with the sun setting around 8 o'clock, we decided to ward off the evening chill with a campfire. Steve and Mike dashed off to help gather wood and cut slender sticks for toasting marshmallows. After we'd had our fill of the gooey sweets, conversation drifted to the explorers who had travelled these same lakes and portages many years ago.

"I wonder who was the very first white man ever to come here," Steve said dreamily.

"There's not much in the records about who was first,"

Dick told him. "The earliest white men were interested in the fur trade rather than history or geography. But in 1659 or 1660 Sieur des Groseilliers and his younger brother-in-law, Pierre Esprit Radisson, made a trip to the western end of Lake Superior and used the Indians' portage routes to explore the nearby regions of both Wisconsin and Minnesota. Their account of the trip was mainly a promotion to attract European investors in their fur trading ventures, and it's a bit hard to tell where they went.

"The first white man, whose visit to the boundary waters area is a matter of record, was Jacques de Noyon who also may have been the first traveler in this area to have been referred to as a voyageur. However, he didn't come through this particular part of the boundary area, having used the Kamenistikwia route, which goes from what is now Thunder Bay, Ontario on Lake Superior to join the boundary route at Lac La Croix, about 25 miles west of where we are now.

"In 1731 La Verendrye used the boundary route on his expedition in search of the 'Northwest Passage' to the Pacific Ocean, the objective of most explorations of Canada and the western Arctic Ocean in those days."

Dick, a history buff, was warming to his subject. I could see the boys were interested but getting drowsy so I suggested they get their sleeping bags. After they settled themselves in comfortable nests curled up near the fire, Dick went on.

"Like the others who tried, La Verendrye never found the Northwest Passage but he established a route and secured it with posts and forts, which served as the main Canadian thoroughfare to the west. During the next 30 years (the remainder of the French regime in Canada) the trade of the voyageur, the professional mover of freight by canoe and portage, developed as a way of life and an essential part of the Canadian economy.

"The legend of the voyageur, his feats of canoemanship and portaging (270-pound loads), his nearly constant singing ('Alouette,' 'En Roulant Ma Boule,' etc.), his picturesque dress, his endurance and faithfulness en.route, and his roistering life between trips, is a unique part of the tradition of the boundary waters.

"In 1763, after the British took Canada from the French in what our history books refer to as the 'French and Indian War,' the English and Scots and some American traders took over the fur trade. They employed the French Canadian voyageurs to guide them and transferred their goods over the canoe and portage routes. The fort at Grand Portage was built about 1768. As time went on, so many traders were competing that the rivalry began to get out of hand. The North West Company was formed as a loose confederation, as a means of self-preservation. It organized the fur trade and established a network which funnelled the commerce of a region stretching from the foothills of the Rocky Mountains to Lake Athabaska in the North West Territories of Canada through the boundary route to Grand Portage. There it was loaded on the big 'Montreal canoes' to be carried over the Great Lakes."

The sleepy pair were now quiet lumps. I doubted they were hearing much but I was fascinated and glad Dick continued.

"This most colorful era of the fur trade through the border lakes lasted less than 30 years. The treaty negotiation after the Revolutionary War did not establish the boundary between the United States and Canada, partly because available maps of the area at that time were so inaccurate that none of the negotiators knew what they were talking about. During this early period in the history of both the United States and the North West Company, the company had reason to believe that its route would fall well within the boundaries of Canada. However, in 1803 the Louisiana Purchase, which included Minnesota, cast a new light on this matter and the company abandoned this route for the Kamenistikwia Route from Fort William (now part of Thunder Bay). Meanwhile the rivalry of the North West Company with the Hudson's Bay Company escalated into a shooting war which ended only with the merger of the companies in 1821. The Hudson's Bay Company, of course, survives, operating department stores in Canadian cities as well as trading posts in the wilderness of the North West Territory and elsewhere.

"Alexander Mackenzie had been a Nor'wester when he had passed through the border lakes in 1789 on his expedition in search of the Northwest Passage. It was then he discovered the Mackenzie River, finding to his dismay that it flowed into the Arctic Ocean. He passed through these waters again in 1793 on an expedition which did reach the Pacific. In the sense that he was the first to cross the continent in northern latitudes, he may be said to have discovered a Northwest Passage. As such, of course, it had none of the commercial significance which had motivated the search.

"The treaty ending the Revolutionary War in 1783 established the boundary as the 'customary waterway.' This provision of the treaty was easy for the diplomats to agree upon and write, but left a lot of room for local disagreements and misunderstandings. The location of the 'customary waterway' was a matter of contention. Many routes had been used and each side argued for the route that would give it the most territory. The Webster-Ashburton Treaty established the Grand Portage route as the 'customary waterway' and provided that the shores on both sides as well as the portages should be free and open to the people of both countries. The specific details were not settled until the boundary was surveyed in the 1920s under the direction of the International Joint Commission, which had been established in 1909 by the United States and Canada. We saw one of the boundary markers today, you know."

There was no response from the two, now fast asleep. We'd have to wake them to get them into their tent, but I was reluctant to break the spell of the quiet evening with history coming alive. I poked at the dwindling fire to revive it.

"By the time they finally got the boundary marked, the fur trading was over and it seems to me there wasn't much need for it," I said.

"Well, by then people were beginning to think about recreation and preserving the wilderness. The Superior National Forest in the United States and the Quetico Provincial Park in Canada had been established simultaneously in 1909 on opposite shores of the waterway. This unique wilderness was then preserved for generations of canoeists."

"Too bad there's so much controversy over how to preserve it."

"There'll always be a hassle between those who place preservation of the wilderness above all else and those who would exploit the wilderness. Those positions are extremes, of course," he added. "As with any controversy, nobody will admit to being an extremist. Actually, everyone involved claims to be a conservationist but each has his own definition. You can expect the controversy to continue with a series of compromises on both sides of the border, none of which will ever satisfy more than a fraction of those who have taken sides."

The fire was beyond reviving and it seemed time to end the discussion and turn in. Dick doused the glowing coals with a kettle of water while I found a flashlight and got the boys moving sleepily up the path to their tent. In the morning we would pack up and return to civilization.

There was a three-quarter moon out now and I snapped off the flashlight. Gazing out at its silvery path across the still lake below us, I imagined the shadowy form of a 25-foot "canot du nord" gliding through the dark waters. Or did I? Perhaps it was the ghost ship of Mackenzie—or La Verendrye returning on his eternal search for the Northwest Passage.

Chapter 7
Sailboats in the Wilderness

Principal Lakes: Seagull, Alpine, Ogish

For map of lakes in this chapter, see pages 14-15.

For new experiences and fun on a canoe trip, you can't beat having a 22-year-old along. From the moment our college son roared into our driveway one warm evening early in July life went into an upswing.

Dicky, as he's always been called to avoid confusion with his father, had travelled over a thousand miles on his Honda 250 from his eastern school on a coast-to-coast tour, which included a stop-off with us for a canoe trip. Kayaks, outboards and, more recently, sailboats had been an important part of his life since the age of five and our tales of our BWCA canoe experiences had excited his interest. Now our nautical son was arriving for a firsthand experience, sails set and tugging at the mooring rope!

We were ready, our gear packed and waiting; Mike was here to spend the night so we would be set for an early morning start. The 12-year-olds had been in high spirits all day, foreseeing extra fun and adventure with a glamorous older brother along. The advantage of sharing the paddling and portaging wasn't lost on them either.

Around noon the following day we picked up our rental canoe from an outfitter on the Gunflint Trail and once again headed for Seagull Lake. Dick and I had decided a repeat of our 1964 route as far as Ogish Lake was about right for the days we had.

The day had become very warm and humid. Little time was lost loading canoes at the boat ramp and getting out into lake breezes. With Dicky at the stern and Steve and Mike paddling bow and center positions, the boys' canoe soon moved into the lead. Dick and I stroked at a faster pace than usual to keep up.

A couple of miles down the lake the boys pulled up at a small rocky island and climbed out. We headed in to join them.

"Snack time, Mom—we're starved!" Dicky called. "What

60

d'you got?"

Thankful I'd stopped for a last minute extra loaf of bread, I produced it from the grocery bag it was still in. "I'll get jam and peanut butter in a minute," I said.

"Don't bother—this is great!" Dicky happily helped himself to a couple of slices and passed the loaf.

Plain store bread was not my idea of a snack but I had to admit it tasted fine under present circumstances—and saved time. The sun's glare off the water was hot and bright and Dick and I were anxious to reach the deep shadowed portage.

"On days like this a portage trail is like an air-conditioned tunnel," I informed my older son.

"Yeah?" His deep set sea-blue eyes crinkled expectantly. "Come on, you guys—let's get moving."

Mike and Steve were already halfway to the canoe, munching bread. We made a last minute check of maps on the portage location with Dicky and shoved off.

The boys had unloaded and were heading down the trail to Alpine Lake by the time we slid up beside the landing dock (a well-built affair, found only on the popular access lakes). I started off with a pack while Dick was hauling the canoe out. It would be a help for him to have only one to carry on this trip. His college son's well developed neck and back muscles, from several years on the wrestling team, would make light work of portaging a canoe.

The woods were every bit as refreshing as I had anticipated. Hardly noticing the weight of the pack, I took my time, enjoying each step. Sunlight filtered through the high leafy ceiling, striking patches of gold among the textured greens and browns of the forest floor. In the silence even the flutter of bird wings was noticeable until two red squirrels began racing games up and down a tall white cedar, yelling insults at one another. Rounding a bend, I came upon an aluminum canoe a few yards ahead bobbing along above jean legs and sneakers. Just beyond, Alpine's brilliant blue glistened through the greenery. At the landing the younger boys were disentangling themselves from packs. I skirted the slow-moving canoe to join them, calling a greeting to my older son as I passed. His unhappy grunted response came as a surprise.

As soon as he lowered the canoe at the water's edge, he stood up, rubbing neck and shoulders with a grimace of pain.

"You okay?" I asked.

"Sure. But that yoke is murder—hits every nerve in my neck!"

Dick had come down to the landing, setting his aluminum burden down beside the other. "We'll swap yokes," he told Dicky when he heard the trouble. "I made mine to fit my shoulders and padded it with foam—helps a lot."

We camped on a beautiful site high above Alpine's waters that night. The boys discovered a rock ledge the right height over deep water for diving and spent most of the evening in swimming.

Breakfast was pancakes topped with crunchy bacon bar crumbles and syrup—hearty and delicious! Wilson's bacon bar, equal to a pound of bacon, cooked and condensed into a 2x3-inch foil-wrapped packet, was a luxury (about double what you'd pay for a pound of bacon in the supermarkets) but one we considered well worth it.

Before shoving off, Dick traded yokes and the boys made sure they had map, compass and pocketsful of dried fruits and nuts in case we got separated. Our destination for the night was Ogish Lake and we'd meet there.

"Don't worry, we won't get too far ahead," they assured us. "You've got the food basket!"

The three soon disappeared from sight among Alpine's islands—but not from sound, their progress followed by the rhythmic strains of "Row Man Row," "Frere Jacques" and favorite camp ditties. It was strange hearing the songs of man across the wild lake where the sounds of loons and ducks, hooting owls and distant wolf calls had predominated through the centuries.

"What do you suppose the rocks and trees think of this?" I said to Dick.

"Fills them with nostalgia for the days of the voyageurs' chants," he laughed.

The voices faded behind an island, then came strong again. The haunting melody of "Little Red Wing" rang forth, although we couldn't hear the words.

"Gosh all hemlock!" Dick burst out, obviously upset.

I glanced back at him in surprise. "Why that's a beautiful song."

"Not the way Dicky and I've sung it. I only know the fraternity version and I'm sure it's all he knows. (They belonged to the same fraternity in college years.) Pretty raunchy for young ears!"

"Oh—well, Dicky wouldn't teach anything like that to the boys."

"Unless he thinks he's helping them grow up," he groaned.

We paddled into the portage landing as the trio were hauling out packs from their beached canoe.

"Great concert!" I called.

"Trouble is we ran out of songs we knew the words for," Steve said. "Dicky taught us that last one."

"It sure had dumb words," Mike added. "Lots of places you just sing la-de-dah-dah."

I couldn't suppress a grin as father and older son's eyes met in a knowing twinkle.

The twinkle was gone, however, by the time Dicky had carried the canoe across the steep 44-rod portage into Jasper Lake. Once again he set the canoe down with a groan. This yoke had been worse than the other. Built for Dick, it was too narrow for his broad shoulders. Yokes were switched again. With the boys' help, Dicky carrying two packs at a time, it didn't take long to transport all the gear. They had become a well organized team, loading and shoving off while Dick and I were still taking our time on shore.

"Hard to figure out how Dicky has such trouble portaging a canoe when two packs are no problem for him," I said.

"Depends on balance more than strength," Dick explained. "The yoke has to rest on the right place—obviously neither of these do, but he'll get used to it."

Whether he would have or not is still a question. Our innovative son had other ideas, we were soon to find out.

There were no voices raised in song this time as we paddled across the north end of Jasper Lake, and we saw no trace of the boys at the portage entrance. Could they have carried the canoe and four packs across in such a short time? It hardly seemed likely.

The rocky trail led to a small "in-between" lake with a portage out its other end going into Ogish. When we reached the shore of the small lake we scanned its half-mile length with the binoculars but saw no sign of humanity or gleam of aluminum.

"They must be lost. . . Do you think we better go back to look for them?" I asked anxiously.

"Gee whillikers! you don't need to worry about those kids. Maybe they decided to explore the lower part of Jasper."

I was sure they hadn't, but Dick was so positive they were okay I tried to relax. We transferred the packs to the canoe and pulled out. Almost at once I heard (or thought I did) faint sounds of voices and laughter coming from the densely wooded shore of a bay on our left. Dick heard it too.

"But they couldn't be there—there's nothing but woods and no break in the shoreline," I puzzled.

"There's a stream!" Dick said, swerving the canoe around with a powerful stroke. "The map shows one."

We were almost abreast of it before we saw the opening, hidden behind the scrubby branches of willow trees. A slight current eased us toward the mouth. We could hear voices plainly now. Maneuvering for a view through the overhanging bushes, we saw them coming—three happy-faced boys in water to their knees pulling and guiding their pack-filled canoe upstream.

"Wow! This is the way to portage!" they called out, catching sight of us.

I had to agree it made sense. The canoe was doing the carrying while the boys were enjoying a wade in cool water. Their 17-foot craft had grounded on rocks and gotten stuck in fallen trees at times, we learned, but obviously extricating it had been part of the fun.

"We met a couple of girls paddling out of an inlet on Jasper Lake who had come downstream this way," Dicky said. "Sure beats carrying the stuff!"

At the next portage we found another navigable stream—at least by a flat-bottomed canoe being pulled. Dick rolled up pant legs and joined the waders (sneakers were kept on because of the rocky bottom) while I disembarked at trailside for a delightful, pack-free hike. As it would take them longer I had plenty of time for observing the small things I usually missed.

Bright orange paint on a sunny rock shelf turned out to be billions of infinitesimal segments of lichen crowded together to form the large splashes of color. At the portage landing on Ogish I sat down to wait on a flat rock in deep shade. The woodsy smells of damp vegetation, rotting logs and black mud arose to mingle not unpleasantly with a dry offshore breeze. Close to my rock the water was dark and motionless except for skating waterbugs darting across its surface. In a sunbathed patch of reeds the fluorescent aquamarine wings of a dragonfly caught my eye. I watched as it flew over a small sheltered bay, dipping its abdomen to the surface at regular intervals—laying its eggs, I later learned.

Before I knew it the sound of voices and glimpse of aluminum through the bushes announced the guys' arrival. They climbed into their canoes at the lake edge and Dick paddled over to pick me up, now an enthusiastic convert to this method of portaging.

As we headed out of the inlet into wider sections of Ogish we hardly recognized it. The pristine wilderness of two years ago seemed to have vanished under an invasion of humanity. We passed two or three campsites overflowing with large groups of young people. Canoes dotted the lake. By a stroke of luck our former island campsite was unoccupied and we gratefully pulled up to its rock slab beach.

While the others set to work pitching tents, I unpacked "kitchenware" and made a survey of the food pack. Large inroads had been made on the bread and snack supplies but dinners were holding out okay. For the evening meal I had brought along three packages of Lipton's beef stroganoff, enough for at least six good-sized servings. As soon as Dick got the fire going, I'd start simmering a pot of dried mixed fruit and he'd probably bake biscuits.

Late afternoon swims helped build up tremendous appetites. The meal tasted as delicious as any we'd ever eaten, all agreed. Outdoor appetites have a way of magically transforming ordinary food into ambrosia. We stuffed ourselves and there was still some stroganoff left in the pot.

"I'll set the pan in the lake with a rock on the lid and it'll keep." I said.

Our large-sized son looked highly pleased. "Then we can run down to the 'spaghetti house' for a bedtime snack!"

How could stroganoff turn into spaghetti, I inquired.

" 'Spaghetti House' is the name of the joint where we go for midnight snacks at school," he laughed.

There was no crawling into sleeping bags at dusk for Dick and me that night. Entertainment was at hand! After supper the boys took the canoe out and returned with a boatload of driftwood and as soon as it was dark they built an impressive bonfire on the rocks. We sat around it, enjoying the warmth in the cool night air. At a campsite on the opposite shore another bonfire glowed and the music of guitars and young voices wafted pleasantly across the lake. It was a deep velvety evening, no moon, but the stars were so bright you felt you could reach up and touch one.

When the fire died to red embers marshmallows were toasted on long sticks and "some-mores" constructed, by sandwiching hot marshmallows between graham crackers with a Hershey chocolate bar slipped in to melt into delicious gooeyness. A pot of water had been boiling for cups of instant cocoa. True to his word, Dicky went down to the "Spaghetti House," bringing back the pan of stroganoff. None of the rest of us could bear the thought of another bite so he finished it off, even scraping the pot!

A strong westerly breeze was stirring up foot high waves in the morning. After breakfast we sat on our rock overlook sipping second cups of coffee (or cocoa), watching a party of canoeists struggling against wind and waves, presumably on their way to the portage at the southwest end of the lake.

"Great day for a sail!" Dick said.

"Yeah!" Dicky nodded. 'Wish we had our boat here."

Father and son had built a small sailboat together during Dicky's junior year in high school.

The two exchanged glances and an idea seemed to grow in both minds at the same time. "Let's make a catamaran!" The words were barely out and they were on their feet heading down the rocks to the beached canoes. Mike and Steve followed, eager to be in on whatever was coming next. How they were going to turn two canoes into one sailboat was a mystery to me. I was content to wait and see, lingering on my rock bench sipping coffee and "lake-watching," with no compunctions whatever about the waiting breakfast dishes. Having the time to break routine and be lazy is a luxury I put in a class far above material things!

The building of the catamaran turned into half a morning's project. It took quite a while fashioning sturdy poles for mast and braces out of deadwood, but locating enough 1/8-inch nylon line to tie them together presented the worst problem. Steve and Mike robbed the tents of every piece not absolutely essential for holding them up while I turned the packs inside out searching for loose scraps, but there was still not enough.

The canoes were held together by two poles lashed firmly across the fore and aft aluminum thwarts. Then a mast was erected between them and a tarp sail tied to that. Finally gaff and boom poles were fastened to top and bottom to brace the sail. It was then time for the launching.

As soon as the two aluminum hulls were shoved off the rocks the smaller boys climbed in, grabbing paddles which they held vertically between the boats as centerboards. Dick and Dicky jumped in the sterns to man the sail and the paddle-rudder. A lug sail (off center) had been devised so they could start off tacking into the wind.

The strange craft took off with a lurch as a gust of wind caught the sail. For a few minutes she plunged out over the waves like a lumbering cow in a pasture; then things began to happen. The centerboard paddles slipped from the grip of their young handlers, the sail dipped at an alarming angle, and the rudder refused to steer. Renewed efforts and a few hasty repairs kept the boat on a drunken course for a couple hundred yards toward the opposite shore. At that point it was necessary to come about or collide with the land, but it was no easy task to turn the unwieldy craft. When she finally swung around and headed downwind with a spirited surge, applause arose from campers on shore who had turned to watch. Dick said later he didn't know if they were being applauded as sailors or comedians!

The catamaran was soon floundering again, however, and by the time shore was reached the ropes had pulled loose, the centerboards and rudder were useless and the mast was dangerously close to crashing. A laughing crew climbed overboard into the surf to keep the rapidly disintegrating jury-rig from slamming into the rocks. Project catamaran was labeled a failure but the venture a howling success!

Supper was a hearty pot of beans cooked with a packet of ham cubes, the rest of the fruit compote and fresh baked corn bread. We had run out of regular bread. In fact, we had run out of almost everything except freeze dried dinners, fruit punch and breakfast foods. I had underestimated the amount of lunch and snack foods necessary to satisfy young male appetites, it seems. Calling a conference, we decided to cut the trip a day short and start back for civilization and food in the morning, which would get us to Grand Marais in time for a restaurant dinner that evening.

The wind had shifted to the southwest by the time we were ready to leave the next day. Dick and I started off ahead, paddling at a good clip with a strong following breeze. It wasn't long, however, before the boatload of boys overtook us, grinning as they swept past under full sail! A tarp lashed on poles was held in place by Steve and Mike, Dicky sat in the stern steering with a paddle.

"Meet you at the portage!" they sang out.

We laughed and waved in reply.

They were waiting when we stroked in to the landing. The four walked the canoes downstream again while I chose to enjoy hiking the solitary trail—so far we had met no one on the lakes. The same plan was followed at the next portage but canoes and gear would have to be carried on our backs from Jasper into Alpine as a waterfall made the stream unnavigable. At least the steep trail was downhill this direction.

Winding through the narrow eastern inlet of Jasper, we came upon an empty campsite on the left bank. The boys' canoe in the lead headed in. "Lunch stop!" Dicky called out, the younger boys taking up the cry. It was a bit early but we pulled in without a protest.

As I dug leftovers and odds and ends out of the food basket and spread them on the picnic table I thought it was a good thing we weren't staying longer. Leftover biscuits thickly spread with jam and peanut butter plus small boxes of raisins supplied the main part of lunch and a can of freeze dried meatballs (with water added for a minute's soaking) provided tasty hors d'oeuvres. No one wanted to go back to the deep part of the lake for water so we dipped up a bucketful nearby. I had some misgivings about its yellowish tinge but pink Kool-Aid improved the color somewhat; except for its warm temperature, it tasted okay.

At first I paid little attention to the boys' laughing chatter. Then curiosity got the best of me. All three bent over their drinking cups and were staring into them in fascination. . . "Hey, look at the little guy go!" . . . "He won!" . . . "Aw, mine are going in circles!"

When I asked what they were staring at, "Bugs." came the nonchalant reply.

"Bugs!"

Steve held out his cup for me to look into. At first I saw a few tiny specks floating on the surface . . . then suddenly I noticed they were moving under their own power! I glanced into my cup. Specks were moving in it too—and I had already drunk half!

Dicky waved his hand reassuringly. "Nothing to worry about, Mom. Adds protein to the diet."

Nevertheless, we all decided to postpone further liquid refreshment until we reached Alpine's deep waters. I'm happy to add that whatever the little bugs were, none of us ever suffered any noticeable ill effects from them.

Setting off single file after lunch down the narrow inlet, our canoe first, we seemed to be making very slow progress for the strength of our paddling.

"There must be a strong current here." I said to Dick.

Both of us concentrated on paddling harder for several minutes. Then I thought I heard a suppressed snicker from behind and glanced around. There was our "strong current!" Relaxed, arms folded, sat the grinning three, the bow of their canoe firmly attached to our stern tow line!

After the hard work of the overland portage on the way in, there was no question about circumventing the long trail into Seagull now. They would paddle around Alpine's extended arm and shoot the shallow rapids Dick and I had previously avoided.

It took quite a bit of time but had been well worth it,

Paddling on North Temperance Lake

they claimed when picking me up later at the landing. By now it was well after 4 o'clock but the 4- or 5-mile trek down the length of Seagull should be fast with a southwest wind blowing strong under a cloud cover. We made plans to meet the boys at the lower end to guide them through the confusing maze of islands.

With their tarp sail again erected and ballooning to full capacity, their canoe slowly churned ahead of us through the rolling waves. I don't know why I felt apprehensive—our older son had sailed in all kinds of weather and raced dinghies at school.

"He knows what he's doing. You don't have to worry about him," Dick reassured me.

Nevertheless, my eye remained glued to the green-sailed canoe setting a trim course down-lake.

By the time we reached the first of the islands it had disappeared into a passage between them. We followed, sure we'd come upon the boys pulled over somewhere waiting, but we saw no sign of them. Then suddenly I caught a glimpse of them passing between two islands some distance ahead. I waved and hallooed, and

69

felt sure they saw us. We hurried to catch up but, when we didn't find them, decided they had gone on, having recognized where they were.

Misgivings grew as we paddled the straight inlet to the boat ramp and saw no canoe, nor anyone on the dock.

"Maybe they've carried everything to the car already," Dick said doubtfully.

They were not at the car or anywhere around when we pulled in. "We better go back and look for them," I said

"No. We could miss them among the islands. Then they'd come in and might go looking for us! . . . They'll probably show up any minute."

We sat down on the dock to wait after transferring our gear to the car. Ten minutes dragged by; 15 seemed an eternity.

"Dick, they didn't have a map or compass." I broke into our silence.

"I know. I've been thinking about that—kicking myself!"

It wasn't until we were well down Seagull that we'd discovered both maps and compasses in our canoe, the gear having gotten mixed up when distributing packs for shooting the rapids. We hadn't thought it anything to worry about then, so sure we'd be keeping together.

"They've no food either—they must be starving," I added miserably.

In the next half hour I found a lot worse things to worry about. My mind conjured up all sorts of disasters—a capsized canoe; boys unable to cling to it, floundering in the big lake, exhaustion. . . . Drowning! I kept trying not to picture the overburdened canoe attempting to tack into the wind, sail lurching crazily out of control, its mast whacking unwary heads as it capsized in the rolling waves. I was sure Dicky would never try to sail such a lash-up into the wind, but at the same time I couldn't stop the pictures.

Worst of all was the responsibility for the life of someone else's son! We had always been so cooly confident of our control over whatever situation arose; we didn't carry life jackets. Dick considered them a dangerous hindrance if you were trying to climb back into a capsized canoe. Steve and Mike always wore their water-ski belts when travelling, which seemed enough for good swimmers.

A party of fishermen paddled down the inlet but our questions about the boys brought only negative replies. It was close to

6 o'clock now—almost an hour had passed. I could stand it no longer. We had to start searching.

"I'll see if I can find the owner of that outboard tied up over there," Dick agreed.

Grim faced, he hurried up the road to a nearby outfitter's and was back in a short time with a swarthy-faced young man I recognized as the proprietor. With a reassuring wave to me, they climbed into the boat and sped down the channel. I settled myself for a long wait, relieved that at least something was being done. In less than 10 minutes since I had watched them disappear I was amazed to see them returning. Then I spied the canoe with the three boys paddling into the far end of the inlet!

"They got lost but they're okay," Dick called out. "They were almost to the inlet by the time we found them—didn't want any help."

The three waved cheerfully as they stroked closer. "We're starved!" were the first words I heard. As the food basket was down to freeze dried dinners and mixes, they sat on the dock squeezing spoonfuls of jam and peanut butter from the Gerry tubes while relating their story.

No, they hadn't seen our canoe in the islands but thought they were following the mainland to the boat ramp and didn't need our help. What they were following was the shore of Three Mile Island! With no map, compass or sun to guide them, they had circled around into the opposite direction without being aware of it until Steve recognized the bay into Shirttail Point where we had camped the year before. They had paddled three miles out of their way! The shore was too sheltering to use a sail on the way back and it was a long return trip. (Of course, as I should have known, Dicky hadn't tried to sail into the wind.) I was deeply thankful my worries had been overblown. It was hard now to imagine them seeming so real such a short time before.

It was 8 o'clock before we finally got a meal that night. When we returned our rental canoe to the outfitter (Janet's, then located at Gunflint Lodge) and the boys were hungrily buying boxes of crackers from her shelves, she took pity on us and made calls into town to secure late dinner reservations. Most restaurants closed early in Grand Marais. After checking into a motel for much needed showers, we topped off our trip with a jolly hour stuffing ourselves on fabulous five course dinners at a very fine restaurant called Birch Terrace.

Chapter 8
House with a View

Principal Lakes: Ham, Snipe, Long Island, Cherokee

Cherokee with its deep bays and many islands was still tops on our lakes-most-wanted-to-explore list, and with 10 days of vacation in August we decided the time had come. We weren't taking the boys this time. But we did include a recent addition to the family, a small Welsh Terrier named Tuffy, not quite a year old, who had developed a passion for canoe rides on our lake at home.

Last year we had started out from the south through Brule to reach Cherokee Lake. This year we planned an approach from the north, beginning at a wide place in the Cross River near Round Lake, winding over to Ham Lake with the help of a couple of portages. We hoped this small, less known access point would mean less people.

It certainly did the day we set out. Until late afternoon we saw no one. After a short paddle the river began narrowing and soon turned into a rocky stream that disappeared under brush. Beside it was a well used portage trail. But not for us! Our lesson from our older son had been well learned and this time I was a willing partner in the upstream hiking project.

It was a very shallow stream at the start and by the time we had gone a hundred yards or so there seemed to be more rocks than water.

"It'll get better," said Dick, the optimist.

We picked our way slowly, pulling and shoving our balky aluminum "pack mule" until its wide bottom finally wedged itself on a flat-topped rock with a bray of protest and refused to budge. Up ahead the stream looked worse before it vanished behind some boulders on the right bank.

"We'll have to go back—wish we hadn't wasted all this time," I groaned.

"Bet there's deep water around the bend," Dick said,

ignoring my remarks.

"Bet there's not," I replied, unconvinced.

He started upstream to investigate, Tuffy splashing happily ahead in the rocky shallows. I followed and scrambled up on the boulders behind him. On the other side were more rocks and some steep ledges, down which a thin current of water ran.

"Give up now?" I asked smugly.

He rubbed his chin. "Yeah—there's probably a good stream farther up, but it'd take too long."

We had to remove a couple of packs to free the canoe and the trek back was as torturous and difficult as the one out. In all about an hour was lost. Dicky sure wouldn't like this, we agreed as we unloaded the packs at the portage landing.

When we arrived at the second portage there was only an overgrown creek beside it so we carried our gear over the 37 rods to Ham Lake. From then on the trailside streams were either unnavigable or nonexistent and our newly learned lesson was of no use. (We were, however, to find it of great help on the South Kawishiwi River the following year.)

Paddling the length of Ham Lake, we came upon a long, narrow rock-slab beach with low level land at the far end, ideal for a campsite. In fact, there were three, spaced in a row like ranch-style houses in a suburb. We settled on the middle one for a lunch stop as it was cleanest. Ham Lake was not within the BWCA boundaries and there was a marked difference in the condition of the campsites. They not only harbored trash heaps in back but cans, snap-tops and candy wrappers had been carelessly discarded anywhere. The remains of a fish-cleaning operation littered the rocks of the first beach we pulled into.

After lunch a short, easy portage opposite our campsite took us across a point of land to what appeared to be a river but was really Cross Bay Lake. For a mile or more it ran a narrow twisted course through marshy land. Approaching a wider part, Dick proposed a detour to Snipe Lake for our first night's camp. "It should be really wild," he said, handing me the map.

I saw a small, three-pronged lake with many islands. It was at the end of a quarter mile long creek on our right, across a 39-rod portage.

"Looks interesting," I agreed. "And we'd probably have it all to ourselves."

He swung the canoe in a right-angled turn where the creek ran into Cross Bay Lake and we found ourselves poking paddles

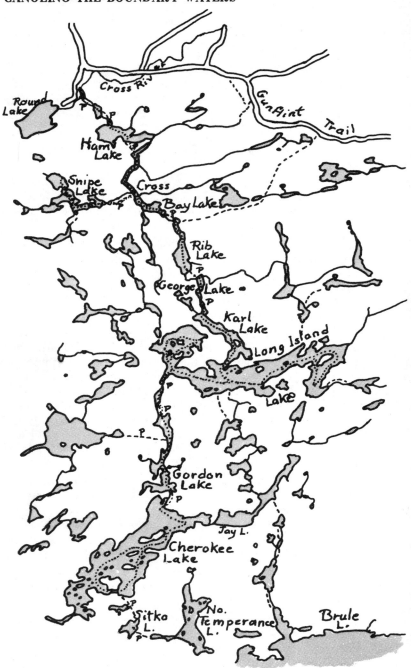

down through a thickly woven carpet of lily pads dotted with white cupped blossoms, which extended most of the creek's length. It was beautiful to look at but frustrating for making progress. The sound of occasional distant gunfire puzzled us, never having seen anyone with a gun or heard shooting in the boundary waters before. We had now passed the border.

Although muddy, the portage wasn't bad. We loaded the canoe at the other end and stroked out into the narrow eastern arm of Snipe Lake with plenty of afternoon left for exploring. High ridges rose above us, thickly covered with pines on one side, bare rock faces on the other. We felt as though we were paddling through a canyon.

"This inlet is part of a well traveled circle route from Tuscarora Lake," Dick said as we were nearing the end. "The main part of Snipe Lake is off the beaten track—can only be reached through a passage somewhere between those cliffs on the right. Bet nobody ever goes there!"

I dug out the binoculars and scanned the cliffs where the opening should be, finally discovering it. We resumed paddling with renewed interest at a faster pace. What we thought·we were going to find I'm not sure. But never in the world what we did find!

Gliding swiftly through the narrow passage, bare walls towering vertically over us on both sides, we suddenly emerged in a bay face to face with a campsite on a nearby island. Two bare-topped, jeans-clad young men lay sprawled on a sunny slope. One sat up to peer at us and immediately dropped back. Then he sat up again and shot a 22 across the lake, twice. Not in our direction, thank goodness! Reverberating against the rock cliffs, the deafening noise sounded sacrilegious in the silent wilderness. Like shooting a gun off in church.

We paddled past with deep, measured strokes, anxious to put distance between them and us as fast as possible. What they were doing on a campsite shooting aimlessly, or so it seemed, we couldn't imagine.

"Perhaps these are guards and the shots are warnings to partners in crime that strangers are approaching," Dick suggested.

"What kind of crime?" I asked, a shiver down my spine.

"Haven't figured that out yet," he admitted.

Whatever their purpose we kept paddling until we found a campsite in the northernmost bay of the lake, as far away as we could get. It was on a small island and cramped but under the circumstances we didn't mind. Even this far we could hear the shots at random intervals during the afternoon and evening, greatly disturbing our enjoyment of Snipe Lake.

We broke camp and left early the next morning, glad to put these gun-happy characters behind us. The day was sunny and hot, but a good breeze kept the bugs to a minimum in the woods and cooled us on the lakes. After retracing our route to Cross Bay Lake, we crossed three well-used portages, though we met no one, and paddled through three small lakes, Rib, Lower George and Karl, from which a narrow passage led into the good-sized Long Island Lake, our night's destination. It wasn't a hard day's travel but time consuming, which our canine companion enjoyed thoroughly, covering far more distance than we on the portages.

She always returned in time to jump into the waiting canoe just before we shoved off and then settled herself on top of the softest pack, from which she loftily surveyed the lakes and shorelines. Cleopatra, queen of the Nile, riding in elegance while her slaves manned the oars!

It was after four when we finally picked our way through a rock strewn channel and entered Long Island Lake. Passing an occupied campsite near shore, we headed out into open waters. The glint of a bare rock bluff about a half mile across on the opposite shore caught my eye.

"Bet I've found a terrific campsite!" I called back to Dick.

He nodded and set our course in the direction I was pointing. Dick was navigator and pathfinder; I the house-hunter and, providing there was a choice and we weren't too tired to care, a fussy one. Sometimes we paddled to two or three, he patiently waiting in the canoe while I climbed ashore to investigate. Top on my list of priorities was a view, preferably a sweeping one from a bluff or jutting peninsula where I could settle with a second cup of coffee for lake-watching. Dick usually joined me. There's something hypnotic about moving water—great for thinking, meditating or just plain sitting. A few moments every morning, or longer if we had time, on our "coffee rock" became an almost indispensable start for our day.

My guess had been right and on top of the bluff we found a vacant "house" with a view that deserved a four star rating! The floor plan included a spacious kitchen-dining-living room, a secluded bedroom nestled under tall pines in back and at the edge of the bluff a sensational front porch facing west.

Dick and I had grandstand seats that evening for a sunset that was a masterpiece. Reds from salmon pink to vibrant magenta reflected on puffy cloud formations above and in the motionless water below. Two loons silhouetted on the rosy lake took turns yodelling, followed by periods of silence. Soon answering calls came from far away, growing louder and birds began arrowing in for splashdowns until there was a well-attended noisy conclave. Ten or 15 minutes later the meeting broke up with races down the lake. Single file they labored into the air and became disappearing black dots on the horizon.

Quiet descended once again, while the scene slowly faded to a pastel seascape in rose and mauve tones. We lingered on the sunwarmed rocks until all light from the reflected sun had vanished and stars blinked on in the evening sky. It was a sunset that would stay in our memories forever.

The morning dawned sunny, a strong westerly breeze blowing up about 8 o'clock. We decided to wash out a few clothes, swim, explore and enjoy our fine campsite another day. We were hanging out clothes when a line of five canoes filled with young teenage girls paddled past our bluff. There must have been counselors but we couldn't distinguish them from the girls at that angle. They were heading east where the lake narrowed for about a mile and a half before winding up in a large, deep bay.

As the girls hadn't returned by noon we assumed they had settled on a campsite; the only other possibility being a route to Kiskadinna Lake through a couple of portages, one of which looked as long and difficult (on our topographical map) as the one we'd struggled over a couple of years ago trying to find Swamp Lake. We set off to explore the eastern arm and bay after lunch, expecting to see beached canoes and hear youthful chatter around each point. By the time we had paddled the entire distance we had discovered two unoccupied, roomy campsites but no girls. Unless they had gone to the bottom, canoes and all, they had taken the portages. It was hard to imagine these youngsters shouldering canoes and heavy packs over such rough terrain.

"Maybe we underestimate youthful vigor," I said.

"Takes more than that to compensate for small size and underdeveloped muscles," Dick commented.

This was clearly demonstrated the following morning when we met a troop of young Boy Scouts and their harried leaders coming out of a rocky, muddy portage from Gordon Lake. Whatever became of the girls we never learned, but we hope they fared better than the hapless boys.

We had traveled from the west end of Long Island Lake down Long Island River on our route to Cherokee and come upon several canoes blocking the portage entrance to Gordon Lake. Some were loaded and afloat, others were on shore or in the process of being launched through the mud. Boys of all sizes were milling around while two men with Boy Scout insignia on their shirt sleeves and disgruntled expressions on their faces stood on rocks shouting directions.

We drifted into shallows at one side to wait. Nearby a short, stocky man watched the procedings from a distance in dour-faced silence. Dick tried to strike up a conversation but didn't get much beyond a "Where y' from?" exchange. We learned that the troop was from Excelsior, which we recognized as a suburb of Minneapolis.

While we rested paddles, a canoe lurched slowly down the trail, carried face-up by three undersized Scouts, looking closer to nine or ten than the required 11 years old. Stumbling over rocks, struggling to keep their balance, they were having a miserable time of it, especially the little fellow clutching the midsection. At one time it looked like he might be crushed when the canoe barely cleared a high rock in the path.

"Tough going for such small kids," Dick remarked in sympathy.

The man nodded but made no move to help or join the melee. Probably a father wishing he'd never left Minneapolis.

Two more canoes without yokes had to be carried laboriously in this fashion; the others had been transported in the customary inverted position, we hoped. Altogether there were 22 people in eight canoes. We didn't stick around for the entire performance, finally finding a place to pull out on shore and squeeze past, but we wondered about the Scouts the rest of the day. We learned from rangers later on that their troubles that morning were nothing compared to when they'd met them the day before, struggling with their gear over a mile of portages from Sawbill Lake through muddy trails and beaver ponds!

By the time we had paddled the length of narrow, twisting Gordon Lake and taken a short portage into Cherokee, it seemed a good idea to start looking for a campsite. Clouds were building and the wind had shifted into the east. We shoved off in choppy waves, heading up a wide eastern bay but found nothing. Reversing directions, we eventually turned south across a wide reach where an island with a heavily wooded shore rising 40 or 50 feet caught our interest. Tucked at its base like a footstool was a tiny round island. Passing it, we stroked in close to the shore of the large island and came upon an opening in the brush and trees. Up on a clearing was a picnic table and fireplace.

"It doesn't have a coffee rock and there's no view," I said disappointedly.

"Looks pretty good though—and we could be getting rain soon," Dick said, glancing up at the lowering skies. He nosed the canoe up beside a solid looking rock and we climbed out.

The clearing was larger than I'd thought and there was a handy stack of firewood left by thoughtful campers. After lugging up a couple of packs, I explored a path to one side and found it led down through woods to a narrow channel, across which was the tiny island. On its rounded footstool top I could see a level place big enough to pitch a tent in a small stand of pines. What fun for the boys—an island all their own! We'd bring them next time. . . . But the best was yet to come.

Back at the campsite I discovered another path at the rear of the clearing. Following it up a short, steep climb, I came out on a rock ledge at least 40 feet above the lake with a view of the whole north end of Cherokee Lake. My coffee rock!

"Come see what I found," I yelled to Dick.

He was as impressed as I when he joined me. My excitement grew as I examined a flat area of rock a few feet back from the edge of the cliff covered with springy sphagnum moss that sank four or five inches under my feet.

"Look—we can even pitch the tent on a soft mattress!"

He studied the area a few seconds. "It's not a good spot. The top of the rock is dish-shaped."

"But we could put the tent at the back where it slopes up. . . Oh, Dick, think of that view from our bedroom?"

"It faces northeast, where the storm's coming from."

"Those clouds could just be passing over. . . Oh, please!"

He frowned at the darkening sky but in the end he gave in. We lugged up the sleeping bag and tent packs and I helped put up the tent, happily dreaming of waking in the morning to the impressive view. By the time we had finished a few distant rumbles could be heard and I had to admit it looked like the storm was coming our way. We hurried down the trail to get supper going. We were in for a race.

Dick took advantage of the stacked wood pile (planning to replace it before we left) and in a short time we had a blazing fire and a pot of stew cooking. If the elements would just hold off a bit longer. . . then a sudden clap of thunder and some large drops of rain convinced us we weren't going to win.

CANOEING THE BOUNDARY WATERS

Stuffing packs under the picnic table and tying a tarp over everything on top, we raced up the hill, Tuffy at our heels, and tumbled into the tent just before the sky opened up. Water soon seeped in through the zippered front end and a puddle grew rapidly. We pulled mattresses and sleeping bags as far back as possible while lightning crackled overhead and rain came down like it was poured out of a bucket. A pond filled the front half of the tent while the two of us perched on a pile of bedding, our knees drawn up under our chins, the pup huddled between us.

"Guess this *is* a bad place for the tent," I admitted sheepishly.

He gave me a wry grin. "If I were the kind of guy who says 'I told you so!' I'd say 'I told you so!' " he said.

As soon as the rain let up a little he waded through the pond, unzipped the submerged door and climbed outside, soon returning with huge handfuls of moss.

"Works like a sponge," he said, dipping a large clump into the water and wringing it out the door.

I set to work with him and it was surprising how fast we had the tent bailed out. It was still raining when we went down the hill to find the fire out and our half-cooked dinner sitting in a cold pot. When it finally stopped Dick got the fire going again and we dined at a fashionably late hour. It was too dark to move the tent so we spread a tarp over the damp floor and hoped it wouldn't rain any more.

Luck was with us. It didn't but we awoke to a gray morning with the threat still in the air. The impressive panorama I had looked forward to was painted in somber tones and viewed through dripping trees. I was far more impressed with the chilling northeast wind blowing across the lake and ready to help move to a protected level spot close to the campfire.

It wasn't long after breakfast was over and the tent moved before Dick succumbed to the siren call of the cliffs across the lake, announcing his intentions for a climb. "Might find a few late blueberries for pancakes," he added.

Having brought along an engrossing book, "Portage into the Past," an account of a couple's trip in the Minnesota-Ontario boundary waters retracing the voyageurs' fur trading route, I was happy to stay in camp. After lunch we'd explore the southern end of Cherokee Lake.

As soon as Dick nosed the canoe into the water Tuffy eagerly jumped in and they shoved off.

The author's husband, Dick, on North Temperance Lake

"You'll be back by noon?" I asked, always a bit uneasy when he went off by himself.

"You bet! With shrimp for lunch you can count on seeing me early!"

A can of freeze dried shrimp was an expensive luxury we included on each trip. Soaked in water 15 or 20 minutes, they are tender and delicious. We had decided upon this treat for today's noon meal.

He had paddled a couple of canoe lengths when I thought of the compass and called to ask if he had it with him.

"No, I won't need it with the lake in view," he called back.

The cliffs were tree covered and shrubby and it seemed sensible to take the compass anyway but arguing did no good. Deciding he was probably right, I retired to the warmth of the tent. The rain hadn't materialized but the air was raw and cold. I curled up cozily on the sleeping bags and was soon oblivious to all except the adventures of the couple paddling the border lakes. My first awareness of time came with hunger pains; I was amazed to find a couple hours had passed. Dick would be back any minute, ravenous.

His canoe was not in sight when I went outside. I hurriedly took lunch items out of the food basket, built a small fire to heat a pot of water for tea and started to soak the shrimp, then changed my mind. They're best eaten right away. I went down to the water's edge for a wider view but there was no sign of a canoe anywhere on the lake.

Going back for the binoculars, I searched the opposite shore for a gleam of aluminum but found nothing. It was well after 12:30—where was he? A shiver went down my spine as I studied the dark wall of trees rising some 50 feet above the cold gray water. Probably he was enjoying the climb and had lost track of time, I told myself.

An hour or so later that argument was no longer convincing. He was lost; there was no doubt in my mind. He didn't have a compass or the sun to guide him and I had no way to go looking for him. All I could do was hail a passing canoeist. Providing I could find one! So far I hadn't seen a boat.

Perched on the landing rock while my eyes scanned the lake, I drank a warming cup of tea and nibbled a tasteless half of a cheese sandwich. It was about quarter of two, and I had gone back to stir up the fire for another cup of tea when I heard a distant call. I raced to the shore. A second call helped me place the sound far down the other side of the lake, but I saw no one. I yelled and waved my arms and the next call came clearer. Then I saw him standing at the edge of a small rock outcrop about 20 feet above the lake and a quarter mile down. I could even see the little dog.

"Are you okay?" I hollered.

He answered something I couldn't understand, so I hollered again.

The same reply, louder and slower, echoed across the lake and suddenly it was clear. "SOAK THE SHRIMP!" he was shouting.

"OKAY. . . WHAT HAPPENED?" I yelled back.

"SOAK THE SHRIMP!" came again.

A couple more tries with similar results and I gave up. It must have been a puzzling conversation to anyone close enough to hear. But at least if food was his primary concern he must be okay.

I opened the can of shrimp, set them soaking and sat down to wait. About 40 minutes later I saw his canoe coming across the lake. There had been considerably more underbrush and rocks to climb over reaching the place he'd left the canoe than he'd expected, he explained, as I mixed a sauce out of ketchup and seasonings, the way he liked it.

The canoe had been pulled up on shore opposite our camp but out of sight in the overhanging foliage. He had become lost when ridges and valleys had hidden the lake, he said, and he must have wandered in circles trying to find it. Even Tuffy had become confused when he'd tried to get her to follow their tracks back. She gave up and huddled close to him. Both of them were frightened at that point. Then finally he had climbed a ridge and found the lake in a different direction than he'd expected and the opposite shore unfamiliar. Pushing his way through the scrubby trees and brush along the lake edge, he had eventually come out on the small overlook and recognized our campsite around a bend.

"Yeah, I should have taken the compass," he admitted. "I was pretty mad at myself. But what made me maddest was thinking of those shrimp when I was so doggone hungry!" He took a huge bite of his sandwich. "At least they taste better than ever when you're starved!"

I don't think we fully appreciated then how lucky we were. Getting lost off the trail alone in this vast wilderness could mean serious trouble and Dick's adventure might have ended in tragedy. Even with a compass, accidents can happen and whether you'll be found or not is a question—one we luckily had no way of knowing we'd be facing in a few years.

We got off to a tardy start on our exploration of Cherokee Lake but discovered a few interesting islands and a delightful sandy bathing beach off a point, remarkable in these rock-bottomed lakes. Supper was late and it was almost dark by the time we'd finished chores and were ready to turn in. Heading for the tent, I noticed Tuffy standing stiff and alert near the path at the edge of the clearing. She was staring into the thick brush, her short-handled tail as nearly clamped between her legs as possible. I signalled to Dick quietly.

"Must be something big behind those bushes!" I whispered, feeling the hairs rise on my neck.

The three of us stood rooted to the spot a few moments but there was no sound or motion in the brush. Dick ventured a few steps in that direction, then started up the path. There was an immediate commotion in the underbrush and Dick said he could feel the ground shake from heavy footfalls. Whatever it was had to be of considerable size to intimidate our spunky little terrier, who wasn't named Tuffy for nothing. At least the animal had retreated, I reassured myself as we snuggled into our sleeping bags, but sleep was a while in coming. Tuffy curled close, pressing against me. Some time during the night I awoke to a loud splash nearby but, as nothing followed, I was soon asleep again.

In the morning the mystery was solved. On my way down the muddy path to the little island I found deep, saucer-sized tracks. Our visitor had been a moose—apparently a good-sized one! Perhaps the animal had been here before, attracted by the succulent roots of the lily pads between the islands and, not to be deprived of its goodies because of mere campers, had returned later.

Coming back from our excursion around the southern part of Cherokee Lake that afternoon, Dick decided fresh baked cake was in order. He hadn't found blueberries the day before but he'd seen a cherry tree near the lake edge. Taking a compass (just in case), he was back in a short time with a small pailful of dark red cherries. It turned out to be such a painstaking job to pit the cherries, he hit on the bright idea of making a bag out of a piece of mosquito netting, mashing the berries and squeezing the juice to use as the liquid for the cake batter.

Whether it was the recipe he concocted or the effect of the cherry juice we'll never know, but the end result could probably have won first place in a World's Worst Cake competition! Not only was it flat with a concave top, doughy in texture and unpleasantly tart, but its deep mauve color was enough to quell the strongest appetite! The cook ate a small piece but I went dessertless.

We broke camp the following morning, looking forward to returning the next summer with Steve and Mike. We had discovered a new chain of lakes as wild and beautiful as any we'd traveled before. In the five days we'd been out the only people we'd seen close enough to chat with were the Boy Scouts and a couple of rangers.

The impression of having the wilderness all to youself is one of the attractions of the BWCA. However, it is strictly an illusion because of the size of the area. There are thousands of visitors every summer and sometimes, as on our next day, you seem to be meeting them all at once.

Chapter 9
Portages and People

Principal Lakes: Ham, Long Island, Cherokee
For map of lakes in this chapter, see page 74.

The sun still showed no signs of breaking through the clouds the day we left Cherokee Lake, but the wind at last shifted out of the northeast and it was comfortable travelling weather. This time there were no Boy Scouts or anyone else on the portages —nobody anywhere that morning, as far as we could see.

"Is this Saturday?" I asked Dick.

"Seems so," he said, after pondering a few minutes.

"Funny thing, how you get out of touch with time, people and everything up here," I said.

"If you want to get away from the world and humanity, this is the place," he smiled.

"Yeah," I agreed contentedly, looking across the empty bay of Long Island Lake—gray waters and skies and islands as far as the eye could see. "But you know, sometimes I almost wish there was a bit more humanity to liven up the landscape."

Perhaps the Mamagwessey heard my wish and thought it would be fun to overdo it. . . But that would be tomorrow. Today the wilderness was all ours. We were sitting high on an open grassy mound eating lunch on an unusual campsite at the edge of Long Island's deep west bay. Not having investigated this part of the lake on our outward trip, we'd decided to enjoy a leisurely afternoon here, spending the night on one of its campsites.

"There must be some good ones on a bay this big," I commented as we glided between a couple of small islands.

We paddled into an inlet looking for a stream Dick thought would be fun to explore but found it too overgrown to navigate. Heading across the bay to take a look at a small rock outcropping on the opposite shore, we spied a good-sized island with a surprisingly flat, low terrain and a short arm jutting from it like a sand bar.

"That has to be a campsite!" I said, my househunting instincts rushing to the fore.

There was no apparent opening in the dense trees and brush covering the island but Dick steered toward it, knowing my curiosity would have to be satisfied. His too, I surmised, as this time he climbed out after me and pulled the canoe up on the extraordinary sand spit.

We discovered a clearly defined path and followed it into a thick stand of cedars. Tree trunks lined up like poles formed walls on each side and, with branches meeting overhead, it was as though we were walking in a narrow dark corridor carved out of trees. After about 100 feet we suddenly emerged in a square opening large enough to accommodate a fine iron fire grate with logs pulled up near it for seats and tables. It too had walls of tree trunks but the open sky provided much better light.

We were at a loss for words in our amazement when we discovered a couple of paths leading off the kitchen in other directions. Small dark corridors like the first, these also emerged into square empty openings.

"Bedrooms—of course!" I shouted. Dick just stood there grinning and shaking his head.

Here was a wilderness house beyond anybody's wildest imagination! Some group must have put in a lot of work—probably had a great time too—chopping rooms and passages out of the stand of cedars. We marvelled for quite a while but in the end decided not to stay. Not only did the trees shut off the view and light but there's something claustrophobic about walls in the wilderness.

It was a relief to get back in the open again; the gray water and skies seemed to have taken on new light. I breathed deeply, enjoying the wide expanse of lake and distant shorelines.

An afternoon's exploring turned up no other campsites, but the rock outcropping we'd seen across the lake offered possibilities for making our own. It wasn't very big and the slope was steep for carrying up the packs but there was a level place on top and a falling-down fireplace of rocks that could easily be rebuilt. Searching the woods in back, we found an open spot under some pines big enough for the tent. We moved in and thoroughly enjoyed our open-spaces lodging for the night. Although our "coffee rock" was only eight or ten feet above the water, it offered a view of the northwest end of the lake and gave us an excellent vantage point for watching a promising sunset that evening.

The promise held good and a bright day dawned the next

morning, the first since the beginning of our trip. We packed and shoved off around 9:30, reveling in the warm sun as we headed out of the bay. By the time we were paddling the long stretch of Long Island Lake we had removed jackets and rolled up shirt sleeves but a good westerly breeze kept the rising temperature comfortable. We passed a couple of men fishing from their canoe near shore and saw two more boats in the distant reaches of the lake.

"It's good to see people for a change," I remarked.

"Guess the sun brings them out," Dick said. "Or maybe the people who started vacations on Saturday are just getting up here now."

Whatever the reason, the parade was beginning. While we were eating lunch on a tiny island in the middle of narrow Karl Lake, three canoes with young people laughing and calling to one another paddled past and we exchanged greetings about the weather.

At the portage landing out of Karl we found a canoe pulled over to the side. Before we had unloaded our gear a young man in his twenties emerged from the trail with a pack which he set down near the canoe. The usual exchange about the weather started us off. Then we found common interests as we had camped on many of the same lakes. Fifteen minutes later we were still chatting.

"You alone?" Dick asked.

"Not this time. I brought my kid brother and a neighbor. They're fishing at the other end of the portage. I usually camp alone though," he said. "Then I bring my raccoon."

"Raccoon! Aren't you afraid he'll run away?" I asked, fascinated—and the conversation got off to a new start. I'm unable to resist the subject of animals, especially wild ones.

"No, he never strays. But he's a nuisance—gets into everything," he said, stooping to scratch the ears of our terrier, who had bounded over, short tail vibrating. "I didn't want to bother my friend with him. . . Only I've done something worse. Forgot to bring coffee!" He stared at the ground with an unhappy sigh.

He had purchased full course freeze dried meals from an outfitter, he explained, taking it for granted coffee would be included. But it wasn't. He himself didn't drink it but his older companion was having a tough time.

Across the portage trail Dick and I discussed our coffee supply and were deciding we could easily spare some when around a bend we were startled to meet a small boy of about 10 carrying a very large fish. It must have been all of 24 inches long. A northern, and he had just caught it in a pool near the landing, the beaming youngster told us when we stopped to admire it.

This was the kid brother, we figured. At the landing we found a tall white-haired man packing up fishing gear. Setting down our loads, we exchanged greetings.

"Haven't been camping here for years," he told us, glancing out at the lake with pleasure-filled eyes. "I came with a neighbor."

We explained we'd been chatting with the young man at the other end of the portage.

"Say, could you use some coffee? We're going back tomorrow and have plenty to spare," I asked.

From his astonishment I might have offered him a gold Cadillac. Then his face broke into a grin. "Golly, that would be great!" he burst out. "If you're sure you can spare it."

The food basket was with us (usually my first load at the end of a trip because of its lightness). I dug out our half-filled jar of instant coffee and poured a substantial portion into a baggie, which he stowed inside a plastic pouch in his knapsack. I've never seen a person so grateful in my life. After thanking us profusely he found some old maps in his pack and began pointing out campsites and places of special interest in this area that we never would have known about. An interesting half hour or so shot by without our realizing it.

Altogether it must have taken us two hours to get across the 28-rod portage and out into Lower George Lake.

"At this rate we'll never make it back," Dick laughed.

"It was worth it though. Besides, the way things go up here, we won't meet another soul the rest of the way," I said.

I had probably never made a more untrue statement in my life. Almost as soon as we pulled into shore at the next portage we saw a small tent pitched at the side of the trail and a boy of about 12 nearby. We were unloading the canoe when a man's hearty voice called a greeting. We answered and looked up but couldn't see anybody. Then I did a double take. Near the tent, stretched full length on a folding aluminum chaise lounge was a very large man clad in shorts and a floppy-brimmed canvas hat.

"Great day!" he sang out cheerfully.

We agreed it certainly was and sauntered over to chat.

"Nothing like camping for getting away from it all. . . Hope it doesn't rain though," he laughed, glancing at the tiny tent.

I could see what he meant. How he and the boy fit into such a small space I couldn't imagine. Then through the open flap I caught a gleam of aluminum and couldn't believe my eyes. Filling the entire inside stood an aluminum-frame cot!

He and his son had just come for a few days, to give the boy a taste of roughing it, he said with a complacent smile. How long had we been out?

"Eight or nine days, I guess," Dick said. "What's been happening back in civilization?"

"The war still on?" I put in.

"Yeah, same old world," he grimaced.

The conversation drifted into the various ills of the world and what should be done about them. It was quite a while before Dick finally hoisted up the canoe and I a pack, and we started across the portage. On the return trip we discussed the comforts-of-home campers. Dick had noticed the cot too.

"I wondered if I'd next be seeing a refrigerator or a TV," he chuckled.

"I feel sorry for the kid," I said. "That's no way to be introduced to camping!"

"Well, there're as many ways to go camping as there are people, I guess," he replied.

The truth of this was to be re-emphasized several times before this trip was over.

There were two more lakes and portages to cross to reach our planned overnight stop at Ham Lake. We'd have to set a faster pace and refrain from any more chats if we wanted to get there for supper. Dipping paddles at a speeded-up rhythm, we propelled our craft down Rib Lake's mile length.

The 59-rod portage at the other end into Cross Bay Lake was an easy, hard-packed trail, being close enough to roads and resorts to attract considerable traffic. It was still three portages away from the access point, however, which is why we found the monstrous blue canvas tent in a clearing at the end of the trail so astounding. Compared to the tiny pup tent, it was a summer cottage! There was even an ell-shaped wing and screened porch! A husky man was chopping wood at the edge of the forest, and playing in the charred wood and ashes around the fire grate were two toddlers being carefully watched by their smiling mother. We waved and called greetings but this time didn't stop.

"At least if it rains, they'll have plenty of room inside,"

I said as we headed out into Cross Bay Lake.

"But can you imagine carrying that tent across portages if it gets wet!" Dick groaned.

The portage into Ham Lake was a short one. After the first trip across we set down our loads near the water's edge and looked over to the campsite where we'd stopped for lunch the first day, glad to see it unoccupied.

"You know, this is the first portage today without people," I said, starting back up the path.

The words were hardly out when a thin young man came into view over the rise. He was carrying a small gray pack and his clothes and face seemed almost the same shade. Heading down the path with long strides, eyes on the ground, unlit pipe hanging from his mouth, he passed without acknowledging our greeting. Then he stopped and wheeled around. "Got any tobacco?" he asked. We told him we didn't smoke. Without a word or flicker of expression he turned and continued on his way.

We passed another silent fellow portaging a canoe and at the landing a second canoe was beached and empty. One of the occupants was already heading for the trail with a pack and the other, with a smaller pack on his back, was starting to pick up the canoe. As far as we could see, that was all the gear the four had. Dick tried to be friendly but I shouldered my load and went back. By the time Dick joined me at the Ham Lake landing both canoes were already in the water and on their way, the men having passed him on the trail.

"Thank heavens they're not heading for our campsite," I sighed with relief.

"No, they're getting back tonight," Dick said. "The fellow told me they've been out four days on a circle route from Tuscarora through Gillis, Gabimichigami, Little Sag and down through Snipe. You know, that means in four days they covered about half again as many miles and portages as we've done in nine!"

"And that's the route we decided against because it has so many long portages," I added. "Of course, with so few packs they had only one trip across—but they looked half fed!"

"There're as many ways to go camping as there are people," Dick reminded me.

Our sunny day was fast disintegrating. By the time we had set up camp and a Lipton ham and noodle dinner was simmering over the fire the sky had become ominously dark. We had planned an evening swim but instead were scurrying around covering firewood and shoving packs inside the tent. By 8 o'clock the spatters of rain had developed into a steady downpour. We climbed into sleeping bags, deciding an early bedtime was a good idea. In the morning the rain would be over. Or so we thought.

When the first gray light of dawn awakened us the tattooing on our roof was still going on. It had to stop soon, we assured each other, burrowing deeper in our warm cocoons. A couple of hours later there was still no sign of a let-up.

"Might as well start moving," Dick said with a sigh, groping for his clothes. "Sounds like an all day affair."

"At least we don't have far to go," I mumbled sleepily. "Let's get off as soon as we can, though."

Dick agreed. "But coffee won't take long—I sure could use some."

With pieces of dry kindling he built a blazing fire that boiled a small pot of water, then died out quickly. We munched cold cereal and raisins and drank steaming cups of instant under a tarp shelter. Tuffy remained in the tent. After a brief excursion out in the elements early in the morning, she had scooted back inside and sensibly decided to remain there.

Breaking camp in the rain was something we'd never experienced before—a drizzle occasionally but nothing like this. We began by packing gear inside the tent, covering the packs with plastic trash baggies and lugging them over to the tarp shelter. Then it came time to pack the tent and a problem arose. Tuffy refused to budge. Calling her did no good. She came out, but as soon as Dick unzipped the door to take down the tent poles she darted back in. Finally when the wet nylon fell down on top of her, she crawled out. For a few seconds she sat with bowed head staring mournfully at her collapsed house. Then, shaking vigorously, she bounded off to the woods, racing back with a stick she dropped playfully at our feet. If she must be out in the rain, she might as well enjoy herself was her apparent philosophy.

We probably set a record that morning, shoving off in something less than an hour. The packs were covered with a tarp and hooded raincoats protected us but poor Tuffy had neither. Perched on top of the wet tarp, she was the picture of shivering misery. I made a place for her underneath it but she refused to crawl in. On the portages she made up for it, racing around in high spirits, even fetching a pine knot once and dropping it in the canoe as we were loading.

She had started this enterprise earlier in the trip, bringing a small rock or stick to drop in the canoe at the landings when we were ready to shove off—Tuffy's souvenirs, we called them. Dick said it made him feel guilty every time he turned the canoe over to portage and her prize dropped out. She didn't seem to mind, however, donating another treasure at the next launching.

The farther we went the wetter both we and the packs became. Below the hems of our raincoats our legs and feet were soaked and we'd given up the baggies on the packs at the first portage when they tangled with the carrying straps. But somehow the trek in the rain turned out to be quite a lark. We sang as we paddled or sloshed over the soggy trails. The rain made moving designs on the still, gray lakes and the woods had a hushed, muted beauty you had to be out in to appreciate.

At the end of the second portage we were amazed to meet a party of three young women unloading their canoe at the landing. They were grade school teachers, off on a final vacation before reporting for school meetings at the end of the week. Long Island Lake was their day's destination.

"We have to make it—we've only got three days," one of the girls said when I remarked it seemed a bit far for today's weather.

"Of course we're nuts to be out in this rain," a second girl laughed. "But we always go to Long Island Lake before school starts. So—!"

We stood chatting and laughing, rain dripping down our faces. They seemed in jolly spirits in spite of the weather and the large quantity of gear they had to transport over six portages. The third girl, stocky, eager-faced, was all business. While the rest of us talked she was stacking packs and pulling the canoe out on shore. Then, placing two paddles crosswise over the center thwart and under the gunwales, she swung the craft up so that the paddles rested on her shoulders, and set off up the trail.

Dick and I were speechless. We had heard of this method of portaging but had never witnessed it. By far the sturdiest of the three, the young woman nevertheless was performing an extraordinary feat, it seemed to us. The other two accepted it as a matter of course.

"There goes Joan. Better get moving!" they laughed, hurrying to shoulder packs and follow.

We could hear their chatter until they disappeared around a bend, and surmised the canoe carrier would join in later. Rain would never dampen the spirits of this remarkable trio!

It was about noon when we finally had the back of the station wagon loaded with thoroughly soaked packs and the canoe tied on top. A beach towel we'd left on the front seat was a godsend.

We took turns, then gave Tuffy a rubdown. Dry shoes and socks helped a lot. It was still raining hard when we started down the Gunflint Trail, the heater going full blast. Luxuriating in its warmth, I thought of the man and boy and the tiny tent, mentioning them to Dick.

"I've been trying not to think about those two," he said.

I tried not to too as we headed for civilization and the small town of Grand Marais where we would dine in spendid comfort at our favorite hotel overlooking the bay. For once I had to admit I wasn't sorry to be leaving the wilderness.

Steve and Mike on cliff campsite looking across Rose Lake. Cliffs of Arrow Lake in Canada are in the distance.

Chapter 10
Boys, Bears and Rapids

Principal Lakes: Bruin, Gabbro, South Kawishiwi River

We had crossed the South Kawishiwi River every time we'd taken a trip to Ely. But if we hadn't been so anxious to try out our newly purchased canoe one afternoon in the spring of 1967, we might never have discovered it. We were driving home from Bill Rom's Canoe Country Outfitters where we had traded our secondhand standard 18-foot Grumman, originally purchased there, for a second-hand 18-foot lightweight. The weight difference was about 20 pounds and the deal seemed an especially good one. Toting our prize home atop the car, chatting happily, we crossed the bridge over the South Kawishiwi some 11 or 12 miles southeast of Ely. I glanced out at the wide expanse of blue water on our left, and suddenly it seemed a great idea to put the canoe in.

Dick agreed at once, swinging the car into a little road beyond the bridge where an arrow pointed toward South Kawishiwi River Campground. We parked near a well-kept boat launch and dug out a map of the area from our pile of canoe trip maps in the back of the station wagon. Dick pointed out a portage about a mile upstream where a winding section of river joined this wide part at right angles.

"Bet there's rapids in that narrow neck—let's go see!" he said, propelling us out from the shallow shore.

There was no current here; it was more like paddling a lake. The Kawishiwi River zigs and zags through wilderness for 50 or 60 miles, its width varying from a few feet to a couple of miles. Even Lakes One, Two, Three and Four are actually parts of the Kawishiwi River.

Before we reached the portage we could see that Dick was right about rapids. We pulled into the landing in quiet water and walked across a point to view them. Roaring white water tumbled over rocks, sending up spray and making eddies where it raced to join the deeper, quieter part of the river. Excitement sparked

Dick's dark brown eyes and I knew he was visualizing shooting the rapids. But not for me—not yet anyway.

Glancing across the turbulence to the opposite bank, we were surprised to see a large tract of cleared property and long, low buildings. A summer camp, we surmised—this was not within the BWCA boundaries.

We hiked the 68-rod portage that skirted the rapids, Dick appreciating the fewer pounds as he portaged the canoe, and set off in calm water at the other end. Our new lightweight seemed to scoot ahead effortlessly. (Probably the lack of gear made the biggest difference.) A half mile of paddling a narrow, bending part of the river with barely noticeable current brought us to a wide stretch of gentle rapids and another portage. We pulled over near shore and sat awhile watching the shallow water splashing over many rocks before we turned around. It was time we were heading home but the South Kawishiwi had cast its spell and we'd be back soon to explore it further.

It was late summer before we made it. Having promised Steve and Mike the Cherokee Lake trip, we took them there in July. Following our practice of trying out new areas alone, Dick and I finally shoved our loaded canoe into the South Kawishiwi one bright August morning. As we neared the first rapids, we saw a large raft anchored on the lake side of the buildings we had seen before. Boys were swimming and diving or stretched out on the float. I noticed they were all in their late teens, about half of them black, and it seemed odd there were no counselors.

"Oh—it's Outward Bound!" I exclaimed to Dick. Recently I had read of their camp somewhere in this area and had been much impressed by their purposes and activities. Giving under-privileged boys from big cities a chance to experience the wilderness and learn how to survive in it seemed an inspiring enterprise. In the course of several trips on the South Kawishiwi we were to meet many of these boys paddling and portaging and find out firsthand the tremendous worth of the program.

When we reached the second rapids Dick decided the 28-rod portage would take less time than attempting to walk the canoe upstream. Setting out on the other side, we had paddled about a half mile when we rounded a bend and came upon a heavily wooded island dividing the river. White water rapids roared over rocks on both sides although most of our view was on the left. There was almost a waterfall there. On shore a thick stand of cedars offered openings beneath their branches where a tent might be pitched—if you could get across the rapids. (On a later trip we succeeded and spent a memorable night, lullabied by the rushing water.) Farther

up the shore a tall lone pine leaned picturesquely out over the river. We reveled in the sights and sounds of the wilderness spectacular for several minutes before pushing with hard strokes through the deep, swift water to the portage on the left bank.

About an hour later we approached the next rapids. The

river had become wide and shallow here and the rock-strewn rapids extended as far upstream as we could see. The decision was to portage. Paddling beyond the mouth of the rapids, we passed a large island and emerged into a lake-sized area that the map showed extending five miles or more. Here we hoped to find a campsite. An island ahead on our right looked promising but a closer view revealed campers occupying it, the first we'd seen today. Another mile or so brought us to campsites facing each other across about a half mile of water, both unoccupied.

The one on our right had a wide expanse of sloping rock while the other offered sheer rock walls to a small private bay and a jutting peninsula overlooking the whole northeast end of the lake. It won "hands down." With a level place under trees for our tent, a sturdy fire grate and picnic table, and "bathroom down the hall," it met all the requirements for our "best" list.

"Let's make it a base camp and take day trips," I suggested to Dick the next morning as we sat on our coffee rock sipping second cups in the warmth of the early sun.

As usual he had a map in his hand. "It's too far from the lakes we wanted to explore," he said, studying it. "I thought we'd camp in an upper section of the river where we could get to Gabbro and Bald Eagle Lakes in a day." He spread out the map on the rock to show me.

He was right. I agreed to move on but held out for a stop here on the way back, if it was available.

A couple of miles of paddling brought us to the rounded end of the wide area, the main part of the river flowing in from the left. It narrowed as we stroked upstream but there was still not enough current to notice. We soon came upon a sign on the right bank informing us we were now entering the Boundary Waters Canoe Area, surprising to me as I had assumed we'd crossed the boundary long before.

"The map shows a small patch of rapids ahead," Dick said. "Can't be much—only a 5-rod portage around them."

We saw the short stretch of rippled water from quite a distance, located in a narrow passage about 40 feet across. Shrubby bushes lined the shore of a small bay on one side and a steep bank rose on the other. We couldn't find any sign of a portage.

"It's probably grown over because it's hardly ever used. Bet we could paddle up those rapids easy," Dick said, surveying them.

I wasn't so sure. There were no protruding rocks and the water didn't seem fast, but as we moved closer I could feel the strong pull of the current in the waves below the rapids. Some wide "V"s where the drop was steepest worried me. "I don't like the looks of those," I said.

"Nothing to worry about—that's where rocks are below the surface. There's plenty of room to steer around them. Come on!"

With a forceful stroke my adventuresome husband swung us out into the center of the disturbed water, eddies and currents pushing at us from every direction. All I could do was paddle fast, hoping we wouldn't capsize. To my surprise we moved straight through, making good headway. But keeping away from the pull of the "V"'s took almost more strength than we had. We came so close to one I could see the big boulder down through the foam just inches below the surface. The canoe could never have cleared it.

Past that, I thought the worst was over but the powerful current seemed to be increasing. We were slipping backwards! I struggled to paddle harder but my exhausted arms refused to cooperate. "I can't do it!" I yelled.

The only answer was an increase in the strokes from the stern. Dick couldn't do it alone. I had to keep going. Summoning a strength I never knew I had, I dipped my paddle at a furious rate. Inch by inch we crawled forward. My aching arms grew numb but there was no letting up. Finally I could see we were going to make it. Not until we slid into a calm bay well beyond the current did we dare drop our paddles. Still breathing hard, I slouched over the bow, letting my arms droop over the sides. Gradually my tingling muscles recovered and I pulled myself upright.

The strenuous episode began to seem funny now and we laughed as we talked about it. Setting off again very slowly—our paddles seemed to have gained weight, we noticed two rangers heading our way. "Everything okay?" they called, letting their canoe drift to a stop at they came near.

We assured them it was but the puzzled expressions on their faces remained.

"We're a little beat—just paddled up those rapids," I said.

The bow fellow turned to look at his companion, then back at us. "You paddled UP the rapids?" he asked slowly.

"We couldn't find a portage so we figured it was the best way," Dick explained.

Incredulous expressions spread across both faces. "No one I've heard of ever paddled UP those rapids!" the fellow in the stern said, shaking his head.

We grinned a little sheepishly and chatted awhile with the rangers before they went on, still looking nonplused. Apparently we hadn't seen the portage, out of sight in the bushes.

"Next time we come we better find it," I said.

"Guess so—but look what we accomplished not finding

it!" Dick laughed.

We picked up paddles, suddenly grown light again, and sitting at least 10 feet tall in our seats, resumed our journey at a brisk pace.

That afternoon we explored an upper part of the river that spread out like a lake. An inlet with a portage at its end led to Clear Lake. We stacked our gear at the entrance and hiked over with the canoe to look around but found its shallow waters and flat shores unappealing. The sun was fast disappearing when we returned to the South Kawishiwi, a gray mist settling down over the bright blues and greens like a shroud. Rain seemed imminent. Across from the mouth of the inlet a wide point offered what appeared to be a makeshift campsite. We paddled over and moved in. A few drops fell while we were setting up the tent.

"Let's get a fire going. I'm starved," I said.

"Okay." Dick pulled a bright orange coated-nylon tarp from its plastic envelope. "We'll try out our new roof," he said.

The rock fireplace and cooking area were completely exposed to the elements. Attaching long pieces of nylon cord to the tarp and tying them to surrounding trees, he strung up a gently sloping roof that served very well in the light, windless showers.

In the morning the rain had stopped but the skies still looked undecided. We thought it wise to leave up the tarp until after breakfast. While eggs were sizzling and coffee water coming to a boil we heard the sound of a small plane, growing louder.

"Must be coming right over us," I said as the noise became deafening.

We looked out from our orange shelter to see a small float plane pass directly overhead.

"It's the Forest Service plane," Dick said. "Probably going to land nearby."

Instead it circled and returned, flying over us again at an even lower level. When we heard it coming back a third time, we raced out on the rocks to stare open-mouthed as the monster roared above, so close I felt I could reach up and grab the pilot's hand!

Shaken—perhaps an emergency at home had instigated a search for us—we awaited its next return. But the aircraft kept climbing, heading west until it disappeared from sight and sound. We watched for it awhile, puzzling over possibilities.

Suddenly Dick said, "Gee whillikers, it's our tarp! They thought it might be a signal for help."

"And when we finally came out on the rocks and they saw we were okay, they went on—that's the answer all right!" I agreed.

We regretted having unwittingly caused trouble but it was comforting to know the Forest Service was alert and ready to come to our rescue should an emergency arise. (At least, those were our feelings then. I'm sorry to say that some years later when help was desperately needed, it didn't turn out that way. But that story comes later.) We hastily took down our bright colored tarp.

The weather was definitely clearing. We set out from camp following the river to a portage into Little Gabbro and Gabbro, both interesting lakes with high shorelines, many inlets and islands. Sometime we'd return to stay awhile but now we had only two days left.

In the morning we started back and, as luck would have it, found our former campsite unoccupied. With most of the afternoon at our disposal, we took a short portage on the opposite bank of the river over to Bruin Lake (called Beaver on some maps). It was a delightful little lake with a campsite on top of a hill and a gently sloping rock beach that was great for swimming.

"Do you suppose any bruins live on Bruin Lake?" Dick asked, amused, as we paddled back to our campsite.

"Could be. I thought I heard noises in the bushes when we were looking for berries," I said.

So far we had seen bears only at a distance, once a mother and cub strolling up a bank across a lake. A few times on portage trails when rounding a bend we'd heard heavy sounds moving off, but we'd never had a close encounter. We wouldn't have long to wait for our first—or rather, Dick's first.

Figuring on only three or four hours to get back to the car, we took our time getting off the next morning. After a leisurely lake-watching session on our coffee rock, Dick headed down the trail to the "reading room," maps in hand, while I cleaned up the picnic table and scraped pans and plates into the fire. Taking the largest kettle, I went down to the water's edge for dishwater. It was too nice a day to hurry. After filling the pot, I sat down on a low rock, enjoying the view across the river and the rhythmic lapping of small waves in the rocks and grasses of the shallows. Then I thought I heard Dick call "Emmy" (his nickname for me from first initials M. E.). It didn't sound urgent but I started back up the path with the kettle.

"Hey, Emmy," his voice came again, casually. "There's a bear here."

I set the pot of water down with such a thud that most of it spilled.

The author's daughter, Pat, portages on the South Kawishiwi River.

"There're two bears. One's up a tree." He was going on in an offhand manner.

I called back something—I don't know what. All I remember is the dreadful anxiety and wondering what to do.

"The baby bear's real cute, looking down at me. . . Now he's climbing higher. Mama's left."

It was an impossible conversation.

He might have been describing an interesting scene on TV. At least with the mother gone and baby up a tree, the situation sounded better. I decided the only sensible thing was to stay where I was rather than take a chance on alarming the mother, who must still be nearby.

After some further description of the cub's charm and finally its climbing down and running off, Dick emerged from the trail, unscathed. When I went back with him I was amazed and horrified at the closeness of the encounter. The tree the bears had stood beside was a mere 20 feet from the open-air john! Dick said the big female seemed to tower 10 feet above him when she rose up on her hind legs. His voice calling to me, purposefully calm, he explained, must have reassured her. At least in the next instant baby had scrambled up the tree and mama disappeared over a short rise in back.

With shaking hands I examined the round holes where the goodsized youngster's claws had dug into the trunk, and looked up to the place where he had clung, staring down at Dick. Probably the bears had been as startled as he. With the sun in her eyes (and poor eyesight anyway) and the wind blowing from behind, the mother bear had come upon Dick unexpectedly, we figured. As he had offered no threat in action or voice, and the cub had immediately obeyed her signal to climb, she had run off. However, a mother and baby situation with bears is always touchy. I thanked my (or our) lucky stars that all had ended well.

Our second bear encounter came the following summer, also on a South Kawishiwi trip. This time it was Steve and Mike's adventure. But first we were to take an unexpected Labor Day sojourn on the river when our youngest daughter Pat came home briefly from a summer job. College was due to start soon and she was eager for a final fling. She'd never been on a canoe trip and it sounded like fun. How about that river we'd been talking about? Steve was pushing for it too, since hearing about the rapids. So off the four of us went.

Shooting rapids was the highlight this time. Though eight years younger, Steve, the experienced canoeist, took the stern position. Pat began calling out left and right directions as they shot over the fast water. His responses were swift and they soon became a smooth working team, never hitting a rock. I'll never forget the exhileration on their faces, especially Pat's. Sometimes they would even walk or line the canoe back up the river to shoot the rapids again.

As I, the chicken one, still preferred to walk, they took turns with Dick bringing our canoe down. A great time was had by all but there was no denying the outstanding runs were made by Steve and Pat. It was a unique experience for both. Even with Mike on later trips Steve was never able to achieve the perfect rapport he'd had shooting rapids with his sister that sun-drenched Labor Day weekend. They still talk about it at times.

The following July's trip up the South Kawishiwi with Steve and Mike marked the beginning of a change. The two had started taking turns portaging their own canoe the previous summer and now at 14 both were tall and strong enough to handle it easily. Paddling the lakes and river no longer presented the problem of holding back so the boys could catch up but of pushing hard enough so we could catch up with them! Sometimes we'd find them coming back over portages after they'd transported all their own gear to give the "old folks" a hand.

"Heck, all the times I've carried your canoe I expected you'd be giving me a ride!" Dick would say.

Teasing kept it fun and allowed them to help without embarrassment.

With the boys along, our pace was speeded up and we arrived at our favorite campsite around noon. No one was there. In fact, we hadn't seen anyone so far, often the case when travelling midweek—at least in those days.

This time Mike and Steve weren't staying. After browsing over maps with us at home, they had come up with the idea of making a separate camp across the river on Bruin Lake for the two-day stay. It being only a short paddle and portage away, they promised to return late each afternoon to eat supper with us. Then the third morning we'd set off up the river together to make camp on Gabbro Lake. Dick and I had gone along with their plans, considering the boys' conduct in the wilderness and attitudes toward safety more mature than those of many adult campers. Mike's parents agreed, trusting our judgment as always when their son was in our care, just as we did theirs when Steve stayed with them.

"Here come the boys!" I called to Dick about five that afternoon, catching sight of their canoe heading across the river toward our campsite. Not only were they arriving to eat with us but they'd brought hatchets to help with the firewood.

It was a merry meal with Steve and Mike enthusing over their camp on the little lake. They had found the campsite on the hill we'd told them about. "Come on over and see it!" they begged.

After a quick cleanup job, Dick hung up the food basket and we shoved our canoe in the water and followed the boys across the river. The tent had been pitched back from the brow of the hill, facing southwest in case of storms, Mike pointed out. It was something they'd learned from the Boy Scout manual. A stack of firewood was piled neatly by the grate and gear stowed inside the zipped tent. A pack containing food was tied by a proper Boy Scout knot to a high branch in a tall slim pine leaning out over the hill. (Grown bears can only climb trees big enough to wrap their "arms" around.) They hadn't forgotten a thing, we said, complimenting them on a good job.

"See you for supper tomorrow," I called as we headed back to our campsite.

Gathered around the picnic table the following evening, making short work of platefuls of spaghetti and freeze dried meatballs, the four of us recounted the day's happenings. Dick and I had explored Eskwagama, a fairly large, secluded lake near the rapids we'd run uphill the previous year. Finding an active beaver colony at its far end, we had spent a few spellbound hours taking turns with the binoculars.

Mike and Steve had hiked a long portage, which started in back of their campsite and meandered a mile or more over to Little Gabbro Lake. We had walked it the summer before, meeting a group from Outward Bound who said they always used this portage. It was a shortcut to the Gabbro Lakes and for the most part had gentle grades, a section of it making use of an old logging road. We left it up to the junior members of our party to decide whether they preferred the portage, which would save three or four miles of river travel tomorrow. The final decision was for the river. A mile or so was a long way to carry a canoe, even taking turns. Paddling was lots more fun.

The boys returned to their camp just before sunset, promising to be back for an early start in the morning. We were tired from a full day; there was still light in the sky when Dick and I decided to turn in. I had drifted into the first stages of sleep when I became aware of disturbing sounds. Forcing myself awake, I realized voices and the occasional click of a paddle against aluminum had aroused me. Just somebody going by, I thought, turning over. Then I heard a canoe scrape onto our landing rock. Dick had awakened too. Hastily pulling on some clothes, we struggled outside, wondering who our visitors were at this hour. A flashlight was now necessary.

Subdued voices could be heard at the lake edge. A canoe was being pulled out on shore. We hurried down the dark path, Dick ahead, then stopped in our tracks, dumfounded. Steve and Mike stood in the glare of our flashlight, their loaded canoe behind them.

"We didn't mean to wake you. We—just wanted to put up our tent here tonight," Steve said. Both boys looked shaken.

"Good heavens, what happened?" I exclaimed.

The two began talking at once. Bear was about the only word we could understand.

"Come on back to the picnic table. We'll get a fire going and you can tell us." Dick turned the beam on the path.

"I'll put some water on to boil if you brought your cocoa," I said. "Ours is up in a tree."

"I think a bear got ours," Mike said.

"You mean you didn't hang up your food?" Dick wanted to know.

"The bear pulled the pack down—part way, anyway," Steve said.

The story came out piece by piece. Apparently the boys never saw the bear. They were singing when they started across the small lake from the portage and must have scared it off. The first thing they noticed was the branch the food pack had been tied to was broken and hanging down at an angle. The rope and knot had held but the pack was dangling waist-high above the ground. Must have been a wind storm, they thought. Then, scrambling up the hill, they saw the slashed-open empty pack, its contents strewn over the rocks below.

There was no longer any doubt what had happened. A bear had been the culprit! Worst of all, by the appearance of things, the robber had been caught in the act and was probably hiding nearby, waiting to return and finish his free lunch. Lemonade mix, sugar, pancake flour, powdered milk and almost everything else was streaked across the rocks. The bacon bar chunk was gone and the baking powder can containing oleomargarine had been badly dented. (In the morning we discovered tooth marks puncturing it—one large enough to poke a pencil through!—but the lid was tightly screwed and the oleo still inside.)

Retrieving their mutilated pack from the hanging branch, there was but one thought in the boys' minds: pile everything in the canoe and get over to us as fast as possible.

"You should have seen us taking the tent down!" Steve laughed.

"Yeah—we yanked it right up off the ground, stakes and all, ran down the hill and dumped it in the canoe," Mike grinned.

"We didn't even stop to fold it. Then we raced back and grabbed up everything else and threw it all in on top. It was starting to get dark and we wanted to get across the portage while we could still see."

"It must have been tough portaging the stuff like that," Dick commented.

"We didn't. We carried it across inside the canoe, upright, each of us taking an end. Good thing it wasn't any darker or we couldn't have found this campsite," Steve said.

"Then we saw you'd gone to bed. So we were going to set up our tent without waking you."

We all laughed at that. By now Dick had pulled our food pack down and we sat around the fire sipping cups of hot cocoa, discussing further points about the night's scary event. The bear must have reached the pack by standing on his hind legs and swiping at it. No one had thought of the sloping hill giving him such an advantage. Even so, he had to have been a big one.

It was pretty late by the time we all got to sleep that night, the boys' tent, pitched by flashlight, close to ours.

"Guess there *was* a bruin on Bruin Lake," I said to Dick as we settled into our sleeping bags once more.

"A frustrated one too. He must have considered the food pack his, free for the picking," he answered.

We heard the boys' voices for a short time, then deep silence. It was good to feel them nearby. Although no harm would probably have come to them, I shuddered to think of the sleepless night they would have put in if they'd been determined to brave it out on their own. It seemed to me they had acted sensibly, with no panic. But I was glad 14-year-olds could become small boys again, wanting closeness and protection. In the morning the roles would reverse, I knew. Once more they would be men on their own and our helpers and protectors if we needed them.

Gabbro was a splendid big lake. We found a breeze-cooled island with rocks and cliffs where the four of us camped comfortably for two days of dry, hot weather. The sun was still out strong on the day of our return. Steve and Mike were stripped to the waist, muscles rippling in tanned backs and arms as they sang to the rhythm of their paddling and whooped with abandon down the rapids. Even I was persuaded to try a couple of runs, replacing the peace and beauty of solitary portage trails with a taste of exhilaration. (It was fun, but my preference still lies with the quiet walks.)

The South Kawishiwi River had now become a favorite route, beckoning for further exploration along its different branches. We knew we'd be back.

Chapter 11
Call of the Not-So-Wild

Principal Lakes: Poplar, Caribou, Horseshoe, Vista, Winchell

What fun the four of us had one bitter cold January evening pouring over canoe country maps. Next summer's trip was in the planning. The boys had come up with a suggestion for a circle route. They would go one direction and we the other, meeting halfway to camp on a designated lake. Warming to the idea, Dick pointed out Winchell, a lake that had long held great allure. The map showed a lake roughly five miles long by a half mile wide, its long northern shoreline broken into interesting capes and inlets. The Misquah Hills, which included the highest point in Minnesota, formed its southern bank, some bare-faced cliffs rising 200 feet or more. (Eagle Mountain, about seven miles from Winchell Lake, has since been officially declared the highest point.) Poplar Lake was the nearest access point, located about 35 miles up the Gunflint Trail, and from there separate routes could be taken through several lakes and portages. One entered Winchell Lake at its western tip, the other near its eastern end.

The more we discussed the possibilities and attractions of this area the better we liked it. Before the evening was over a decision was made for a trial run over a few of the lakes and portages on the Memorial Day weekend.

Two lakes and portages beyond Poplar Lake was as far as we went on our May holiday trip but it was enough to whet our appetites for the summer expedition. We set forth one morning in early August, leaving our station wagon at a Poplar Lake outfitters', from whom we rented the boys' canoe. All of us travelled together as far as Caribou Lake, where we had made camp in May. From here the boys would cross a portage at the northwestern tip over to Meads Lake while our route would take us across a portage at the southeastern end to Horseshoe Lake. The flexible plan was to meet on the second or third day, which allowed time for exploring lakes off the beaten track while en route.

We ate lunch together at a campsite on Caribou, hungrily munching pressed ham sandwiches on fresh sesame buns (first day fare) while discussing how long we thought it was going to take to find each other on a lake five miles long that none of us had ever been on before.

"Got your moose horn?" I asked Steve.

"Right here," he nodded, showing me a bulge underneath a pack strap.

"We'll find you," I laughed.

The "moose horn" was actually the curved horn of a Texas steer fitted with a mouthpiece. We had bought it as a fun gift awhile ago. Both Steve and Mike were cornet players in the school band and could produce loud, mournful wails from the horn (which I had teasingly described as the call of a lovesick moose). This was the agreed-upon signal to help us find them on Winchell Lake. Ours was the bright orange tarp to be hung near the water's edge on our campsite—lowering it in case of an airplane!

After a final check of small essentials: maps, compass, first aid kit, etc., the boys shoved off with happy shouts of "See you!"

"They're sure eager to be on their own," I said, watching them move swiftly away with long, measured strokes. I smiled but was a bit apprehensive. "Do you really think they'll be okay?"

Dick stared after the disappearing canoe. "Well, I'll tell you," he said slowly. "Anybody needing help would be a lot better off in the boys' hands than ours."

I pondered this a moment. "You mean because they passed their Red Cross senior life saving at camp?"

He nodded. "And what about their first aid merit badges? That emergency aid course they took under Dr. Olson was a tough one," he reminded me. "They're really living up to the 'Be Prepared' motto—probably safer on their own than we are!"

It was a new thought and we chuckled a little discussing it. We had no way of knowing, of course, that before this trip was over the Boy Scout motto would be put to a real-life test.

Our destination that day was Vista Lake, not on the Winchell Lake route but within the Misquah Hills. We decided to add it to our agenda as it was only a short distance from Horseshoe Lake. Under a cloudless sky we paddled out into the star-shaped northern end of Vista, heading south. As we rounded a bend we came upon a blue bay sparkling like a sapphire at the foot of surrounding deep green hills. There were no shoreline cliffs, but a

steep rock ledge on an island to our left invited investigation. Circling its lower end, we discovered a gentler slope on the other side. A path led up to a campsite beneath some huge old pines. Excited, we beached the canoe and climbed the path among a grove of trees. Some were so big our hands didn't come near touching when we stood on opposite sides stretching our arms around.

"This one must be more than 200 years old," Dick estimated, staring up into the needly canopy of the towering giant.

I was already at the top of the ledge, marvelling at the view, calling impatiently for him to join me. There was no question about camping here. We moved in and spent the rest of the day exploring. One trail led down the other side of the ledge to a small campsite across the island. Another we followed to a rocky overlook on a northern point, from which a path wound down to a sheltered cove. Ideal for swimming; there was even a diving rock at the right height. The boys would like this, I thought. They could stop here on their way back.

Later in the afternoon we hiked across the portage to Misquah, a small pear-shaped lake deep in the hills south of Vista. On the opposite shore from the portage landing rose a bare-faced cliff whose ledge was at least 150 feet above the water level. Below it a tumble of rocks formed a steep slope to the shore.

"The glacier probably left that cliff sheer to its base but repeated freezing and thawing of water in its cracks has spalled off that pile of rocks," Dick said. "The process is still going on after 10,000 years."

We stood silent a few minutes absorbing the pristine beauty of the tiny lake. There was no sign of a campsite or anything man-made to mar the splendor.

Sunshine greeted us again in the morning but a strong southwest wind was not the best news. We would be paddling into it most of the day. Horseshoe, Gaskin and Winchell Lakes had long east-west stretches. Portages offered a welcome relief but wouldn't be easy with a 66-foot rise on the one out of Horseshoe and an 86-foot crest between Gaskin and Winchell.

Both turned out to be well used with solid footing and enough canoe rests along the way to ease the portaging. We were tired, however, when we set forth on Winchell and bucking the wind and big waves was hard work. A mile or so of strenuous paddling and my arms and shoulders were begging to quit. We had passed a couple of campsites that were small openings on the flat wooded north shore. Steep hills and cliffs on the south shore were intriguing but prevented any chance for camping. There was no sign of the boys or any other canoeists as we fought our way slowly up-wind. Finally we rounded a wide point and discovered a campsite on a narrow peninsula with such a splendid view of the entire western end of the lake that we forgot our tiredness. Food was first on our minds and Dick got a fire going as soon as we moved in.

While supper simmered in a pot we tied the bright orange tarp to trees, as close to the end of the rocky point as we could get it. By then the wind had dropped considerably but it still flapped like a bright flag. With binoculars I searched the end of the lake but saw no people or boats anywhere.

"Bet the boys haven't made it yet or we'd be hearing the moose horn," I said, trying not to sound anxious.

"Don't be too sure—there's a big stretch of water beyond this island."

We were cleaning our plates of second helpings when I thought I heard a couple of short blasts. Then came the familiar mournful wail, far off but unmistakable.

"The boys are here!" I leaped to my feet and raced down to the rocks. Straining my eyes, I could barely make out a speck in the west, which the glasses disclosed was Steve and Mike. The "call of the wild" kept coming at intervals. Then finally the exuberant two were paddling into our cove.

It was a happy, noisy reunion. They were camped down near the end of the lake, they said, had arrived yesterday evening. Yes, it had been a good trip. The portages were pretty rough but they'd had fun. As soon as they spied our tarp they'd started calling on the horn and heading here. Our campsite was pretty great but theirs was even better, they insisted.

"You had dessert?" Steve asked suddenly, a gleam in his eye.

"No, not yet," I said. "Come on up—we've got plenty of cookies."

He grinned. "How about apple pie?"

"Sorry, fresh out," I laughed.

"No, you come over to our place for apple pie."

"Sure. You want us to bring the ice cream?"

"Mom, I'm serious. I cooked a pie."

When I tried to pin him down on details all he'd say was, "Come on over and see." Finally we promised to come as soon as we put the food away and hung it up.

The apple pie was delicious! Baked in a pot lid, it was

The author's son, Steve, and his friend, Mike Randall, were frequent companions on canoe trips. Tuffy is in the stern with Steve.

none the worse for having been hung up in the food pack awhile. The crust was made from biscuit mix and oil, the cook said, and filled with apple slices (dried) which had first been boiled with sugar. Cinnamon, sugar, flour and gobs of margarine made the crunchy, sweet top. We ate huge slices, singing its praises.

"You must have known the trick of keeping a hot fire," his father said, munching appreciatively.

Steve gave him a knowing grin. "Learned it from the best!"

The boys were right about the campsite; it had everything. A wide sloping rock beach extended out into the lake for a sweeping view. On one side was a deep swimming cove. In back a sharp drop formed walls for a cooking area and a path led to a shady open place under trees where Mike had pitched his tent. He showed us the lightweight little "pop-up" he'd persuaded his sister to loan him.

"Too small, though—I should have tried it out at home first," he said. "Steve's been sleeping out on the rocks."

113

"It's really great out under the stars. Glad I tried it," Steve said. "I only put up a tarp if it looks like rain."

He showed us a ledge where a rock wall a foot or so high formed a natural back. A tarp strung from the top made an ideal lean-to.

Before we left that evening, plans were made to meet on Cliff Lake around 2 o'clock the following day. It was a small lake across from the boys' camp, reached by two short portages with a little lake called Wanihigan (on some maps, Trap) in between.

"We'll probably get there first," Mike said. "But you'll find us okay—we'll be near the portage."

"Yeah, we were over there taking a look. There's a real good cliff to climb," Steve said.

"Well, be careful," Dick warned. "There're lots of loose rocks in this kind of terrain."

The weather held good. We set out for Cliff Lake in bright sunshine with a pleasant southwest breeze. Paddling close enough to the boys' camp to make sure that their canoe was gone, we headed across the lake for the little inlet where the map showed the portage.

"They're probably climbing the cliff by now—we're a little late," I said as we pulled up to what had once been a landing dock there.

Dick hauled the canoe out on shore and swung it up on his shoulders while I started up the trail. Then I stopped, my breath catching in my throat. Coming slowly down the path in soaking wet jeans and a very bloodied T-shirt was Steve. Behind him, carrying the canoe, was a grim-faced Mike.

"What happened?" I gasped. Then, noticing the palor under Steve's tan, "Come sit down," I said quickly, motioning to the old pier.

With the canoes beached near shore, the four of us sat on old rotting beams at the water's edge while the story unfolded.

"I got hit by a rock," Steve began slowly.

"It was as big as two basketballs squashed together—like a watermelon," Mike added.

Steve ducked his head, indicating an area under his hair at the base of his skull. "It bled a lot but it's okay now. Mike washed it."

Examining it gingerly, I found a sizeable gash but it looked clean.

"What were you doing—climbing close together?" Dick asked. "I warned you about loose rocks."

"No. Mike wasn't anywhere near me," Steve said. "He was up on top of a cliff. I was on another ridge, about 50 or 75 feet away. I was climbing down from a ledge with about a five-foot drop, facing out, leaning on my elbows. As I slid down, my elbow dislodged a rock which tumbled down after me. It hit my head and shoulder and I started yelling."

"I didn't know if he was hollering for fun or what," Mike put in.

"I could hear Mike calling 'You all right?' and I yelled back 'No!' The blood was running down my neck and all over my shirt."

"I got to him as fast as I could," Mike explained. "But piles of loose rocks below the cliff made it slow going. Steve had got himself down to the lake edge by the time I got there. He was sitting slouched over, limp like he was going to fall. I saw all the blood and thought he might be passing out so I got him into the water, sitting in it up to his neck. I could see the cut had stopped bleeding and I just kept dowsing water on it."

"I don't remember anything about the last part of getting down the cliff. I must have blacked out," Steve said. "The water made me feel a lot better, except my shoulder was hurting so much I didn't think I was going to be able to paddle. After we got in the canoe Mike did the paddling."

His companion nodded. "Yeah. I was getting pretty worried, wondering how we were going to get all the way to Poplar Lake. Then he tried paddling crossing Wanihigan Lake and I guess it wasn't too bad."

"It doesn't hurt much any more—just sore," Steve said.

His color was slowly returning and he assured us he felt all right but we decided to leave for civilization in the morning, in case any problem should develop. The rest of the afternoon and evening we spent with the boys on their campsite. Steve was eager for a swim as soon as we got there and, with all of us keeping watch, we didn't think any harm would be done. At least his cut would get a thorough washing in clean lake water. It must have been the right treatment as the wound healed quickly and never gave him any trouble afterward.

Talking about the accident during supper, we all agreed that Steve was lucky. A falling rock that size could have been lethal. He was also lucky to have a level-headed companion to come to his immediate aid. Before we left for our campsite that evening I posed a question I'd been thinking about to Mike.

"What would you have done if Steve had been knocked unconscious and you couldn't revive him?"

Dick must have had it on his mind too. "And supposing it had happened when you two were off on your own those two days?" he added.

Mike shrugged, his level blue eyes looking from one to the other of us. "Well, where he could be moved, I'd have carried him over the portages, 'fireman's carry'," he said simply. "Then gone back for the canoe and gear. It wouldn't have been easy but I'd have made it okay."

Dick and I exchanged glances. There was no doubt in our minds that he would have. Or that Steve would have, were the situation reversed.

Overnight the weather changed. Sultry skies and a rising east wind greeted us when we emerged from the tent next morning.

"Wouldn't you know—we'll be bucking the wind again," I said disgustedly, thinking of the long paddle down Winchell Lake.

We had decided to break camp and leave after breakfast by the route Dick and I had taken; it was the shortest and easiest. The boys would stop for us on the way so we'd be travelling together. We saw their canoe coming while we were loading at the lake edge. Steve said he felt fine and his shoulder wasn't bothering him. It still seemed wise to stick to our plans, however, making one overnight stop. Our young companions had had enough adventure for one trip. Or so we thought.

By the time we made a lunch stop on Gaskin Lake the wind had died completely and the air hung heavy under a hazy sky. I had seldom felt so uncomfortatbly hot in the lake country. When we finally had completed the trips across the portage into Horseshoe Lake and shoved off, I was ready to settle for the nearest campsite. We found a suitable one at the bend of the lake but the swimming wasn't good and the boys were anxious to go on to the Vista Lake campsite we had enthusiastically described. As Steve seemed completely recovered, we agreed to their going on alone. We'd meet at our campsite the next morning and make the final part of the trip together.

Dick and I took a long time setting up camp that afternoon, moving slowly in the oppressive humidity. Dark clouds were gathering by the time we got our cook-fire going. Lightning streaked and thunder rumbled in the distance.

"Hope we get supper before the storm breaks," I said, moving the pot of tomato sauce over a hotter part of the fire. Spaghetti was boiling in the big kettle.

Dick shoved in more kindling. "I think we'll make it," he said, "but we may end up eating in the tent."

The sky blackened rapidly, casting an eerie greenish light over the lake and land. Not a leaf stirred. Then all at once the storm was upon us. We heard the roar of wind and saw the bending of trees across the lake first. A bolt of lightning cracked close by and rain started falling in big drops. By the time we had scooped up heaping platefuls of spaghetti and sauce and raced to the tent it was pouring. Dick braved the raging elements once to bring the pot of boiling water for coffee. Everything else needed had been stowed in the tent ahead of time, along with packs and gear.

"Hope the boys got their meal before this hit—Mike's tent is so small," I said anxiously.

"Don't worry about them. They probably ate a long time ago—you know their appetites."

The storm kept up most of the night, wind-driven rain lashing the tent and gusts billowing the sides at times. The ropes strained but the stakes held. Dick had pitched the tent on high ground with a good run-off; the inside stayed dry.

In the morning the rain had stopped and, except for the dripping trees, all was quiet. A few broken branches littered the ground but no trees had fallen and our food basket, hung high, was okay. My mind was on Mike and Steve as we went about breakfast and packing. I hoped the storm hadn't been so severe where they were. In any case, they probably hadn't slept very well in the cramped tent.

As we were taking down our sopping tent I heard a sound in the distance that could have been their horn. We stopped to listen and soon the mournful wail repeated. Short blasts followed, then a long call again, getting closer; it sounded like they were having fun. Leaving Dick to finish packing the tent, I hurried to the lake edge and found the canoe rounding the bend. The boys called and waved as soon as they spotted me.

"We had a bad storm here last night. Did you guys get it too?" I asked as soon as they pulled up on shore.

"Yeah, trees down all over the campsite. A real big one fell right next to my tent," Mike said.

"A huge Norway I had my tarp tied to cracked off about ten feet above the ground," Steve said. "Sure lucky it fell the other way."

I stared from one earnest face to the other, not wanting to doubt their word, but it seemed a pretty tall tale. They didn't act excited or upset.

"No trees went down here," I said tentatively.

"Well, they sure did where we were—lots of them, a couple of great big ones. We had a hard time getting down through the mess to the canoe this morning," Mike said. "Lucky we had it in a safe place."

"We didn't cook breakfast, Mom; the fire grate was buried under trees. We lost half our cook set—plates, cups, silverware and a pot must have blown into the lake. Couldn't find them anyway."

My son was looking at me unblinkingly but he's an expert at pulling my leg when he wants to. I still wasn't sure.

"Steve, I can believe the wind blew down some trees and you lost a few dishes but I can't believe you slept out under a tarp in a storm like that!"

"Yes I did," he insisted.

"Yes he did," Mike echoed. "And he stayed a lot drier than I did. I was bailing out that darn tent all night long!"

Dick had come down and was listening to the story. I could see that he believed them. It was impossible not to as they went on.

"I had my tarp tied to a log close to a three foot wall on one side and a couple of Norway pines on the other. It was the biggest one that cracked off and fell." Steve explained. "There was so much wind and rain I couldn't hear it over the noise of the storm. A couple of times I climbed out of my sleeping bag to go see how Mike was doing. His tent was pitched farther back."

"It was protected by a five or six foot wall but the roof leaked and rain kept coming in over the bottom of the door. My sleeping bag and everything got soaked," Mike said unhappily.

I glanced at Steve. "You must have been even wetter, with just a tarp."

"No. My ledge was slanted enough so the rain ran off. I'd stuffed my sleeping bag inside a big trash bag and at least the bottom part stayed dry. We kept hollering to each other and checking all night. There wasn't any way to stay together. The tent wasn't big enough for two of us and there wasn't room for Mike under the tarp."

"The big shock came in the morning when we got up,"

Mike said. "We couldn't believe all those trees down—hadn't heard any in the night because of the noise. Boy, when I saw that big one right beside my tent, it sure was scary!"

"We climbed around through the wreckage this morning counting trees down—37 on the island." Steve looked over at Mike. "And ten on the portage, I think."

"Yeah," Mike nodded. "At first it didn't look like there was any way we could get through. Trees were across the landing—mostly "popples"—in a big pileup. Finally we pushed the canoe up onto the pile upright and kept shoving it forward best we could while we climbed over the tangle of branches with the packs. Then we'd portage a few yards and have to go through it all over again."

Their story had the ring of truth. I no longer doubted them. Yet it became harder and harder to believe as we paddled and portaged our way back to Poplar Lake without seeing a single recent blow-down.

It was while we were feasting on extra-sized hamburgers and milkshakes at a wonderful little restaurant on Poplar Lake known as Trail Service that we learned of the destruction the big storm had wrought. Later we saw a wide swath of downed trees along the Gunflint Trail, men clearing the road, and decided we'd better report the damage on the Vista Lake campsite and portage.

The four of us went into Gunflint Outfitters in Grand Marais. We were met by the owner and operator, a well known and highly respected "rugged individualist," who had canoed and camped a lifetime in the Boundary Waters Canoe Area. She listened intently as Mike and Steve told their story, quietly producing a map and spreading it on the counter.

"We had a tornado here," she said when they finished.

I think we all gasped in unison.

"I thought northern Minnesota never had tornadoes," I said weakly.

"Well, it did last night. Official report. See—here's where it went." With her pencil she pointed out the path on the map, stopping it at Vista Lake.

"Yep, just what I thought," she said, respect in her gray eyes as she glanced up at the boys. "The tornado went straight through your camp, fellas!"

Chapter 12
Changes: For Good and Otherwise

Principal Lakes: Vista, Gaskin, Kiskadinna, South Kawishiwi R.

For maps of lakes in this chapter, see pages 96-97 and 110.

Climbing around, over and under fallen trees, we laboriously made our way to the top ledge of the Vista Lake island and stared around us. At least a dozen big trees were down, two of them the giant Norway pines we had admired so much on our overnight stay here the summer before. Now their huge trunks lay prone, the top branches of one drowning in the lake. The whole southeastern slope, where the path to the campsite had been, was blocked. A large slice was sawed through one of the trunks to allow passage. Many smaller trees and branches had been cleared by a work crew but more clearing was needed to make the campsite usable again.

For several minutes neither of us could speak, appalled at the devastation.

"How did the boys ever survive that night?" I finally voiced the thought in both our minds.

Dick shook his head somberly.

"Your 'Lucky Star' must have been watching out for them," I said with a little shiver.

"They had to have had their own Stars to have come through this," he said.

We pushed through thick branches of a fallen pine where the cooking area had been; I could see the grate squashed beneath the heavy trunk.

Dick pointed to the broken-off stump of one of the giants on the back side of the ridge. "That must have been the tree Steve had his tarp tied to."

Farther back we found a downed pine near a sheer rock wall. "Probably the one that fell beside Mike's tent," I said.

We had planned to have lunch here but neither of us felt like eating. Making our way back down the slope, we stopped beside the freshly cut trunk of the largest Norway. Dick squatted to count the rings. I went on to wait in the canoe, more than ready to leave the depressing scene.

"I lost track of the exact number but the tree was more than 230 years old," Dick said as he pushed us out from shore.

Our campsite was on Gaskin Lake. Luckily in planning the trip, we had decided against trying to camp here, not knowing what to expect or whether we could get through the portage. The latter we had found well cleared, however. Downed trees and branches had been stacked high on both sides of the trail, towering several feet above us at one point.

As we paddled back to the portage after leaving the wreckage on the campsite, we thought of the way Steve and Mike had found it that morning after the storm. The pileup of fallen trees at the landing must have appeared insurmountable. Now we had some real understanding of the work it took to get through.

The boys were much on our minds and we missed them. We were alone on this trip, as we probably would be from now on. Both had attained driver's licenses in the spring and we had promised them the use of our station wagon for a canoe trip between the end of summer jobs and the start of school.

One of the purposes of our return to the Poplar-Winchell area this summer was to explore some of the lakes we had missed the previous year. Hensen, Omega and Kiskadinna, long narrow lakes strung out west of Gaskin, were on our itinerary for the next day. The first two had been on the boys' route last summer. They had mentioned nothing special except a campsite on a high bluff above a weedy inlet about midpoint on Hensen.

Setting off from our campsite early in the morning, we stopped there for lunch, enjoying the view and a cooling breeze on this hot July day. Below us we watched a mother merganzer keeping a wary eye on six or seven downy babies feeding among the reeds. Omega Lake, next in line, we found appealing with its high hills and deep bays but Kiskadinna was to hold the greatest interest for us that day. Not because of the lake itself—narrow, straight with low shores—but because of evidence of a little drama we happened upon.

We were becoming hot and bored paddling Kiskadinna's breezeless length and about to call it a day and turn around when I saw what might be a campsite ahead. "Let's pull in and have some lemonade before starting back," I suggested.

Dick readily agreeing, I scooped up a pail of water and we stroked in to shore. The campsite was as flat and uninteresting as any we'd seen—a hole in the brush surrounded by short scrubby pines. "Who would want to camp here?" I asked.

"Parties coming over the long haul from Long Island Lake are probably glad to find this place," Dick said. "It's about halfway on the Winchell-Brule route."

"Well, I guess somebody stopped here—and left something behind," I said, pointing to a white mound beside a rock a few yards behind us.

It turned out to be a large plastic bag, in good condition, carefully closed with a twister. The soft, bulky contents didn't appear to be garbage. Nevertheless, we opened the bag carefully and peered inside. To our surprise we discovered several clear plastic bags partially filled with camping staples: flour, cornmeal, powdered milk, sugar, and some instant orange drink mix.

"How awful when they discover all this missing," I groaned.

"Maybe they'll come back. They couldn't have been gone long or animals would have been into the stuff," Dick said.

We were putting everything back when I discovered a piece of paper with handwriting on it lying on the ground. "To whoever left this," it said. "In case you come back for your food, we apologize for helping ourselves. We need it desperately or wouldn't have taken any. This should teach you to take better care of your food supplies! Hope you get along all right." The note was signed and dated the day before.

It seemed too late for anybody to be coming back for it now but we left the bag as we found it with the note inside. If no one else came along, at least animals would benefit.

"I don't know whether to feel sorry for the campers who forgot the food or glad for the ones who 'desperately needed it'," Dick said as we climbed back in the canoe.

"Food makes such a difference," I said. "Whether a trip is good or bad, how long you stay, where you go."

Sometimes even where you'll spend the night, we were soon to learn. It was after five by the time we came over the portage from Hensen Lake and pushed the canoe out into Gaskin. A middle-aged couple was fishing nearby in the cove.

"Any luck?" Dick asked to be friendly.

"No, but we better have some pretty soon or we won't

eat," the woman said dourly.

"Can you tell us where they're biting around here?" the man asked in a patient voice.

We confessed we didn't know.

"They told us fishing was good everywhere in these lakes," the woman complained. "So I didn't bring anything for supper."

The man looked unhappy. "Maybe we should portage over to Hensen Lake—we were going to camp there anyway."

The woman kept her eyes on her line. "We're staying till we get a fish," she said.

"Gosh, if our campsite weren't so far down the other end of the lake I'd have been tempted to invite them to supper," I told Dick as we paddled off. We never did learn how the argument ended but sometimes wondered if they spent the night sitting in their boat.

It was at dusk that evening when we saw the beavers. Our meal had been late and the sun had gone down by the time we finished chores and could relax on the rock ledge at the edge of our campsite. We were admiring the soft sky colors and reflections in the gently rippled lake when I noticed two small brown heads making "V"s in the water between our island and the shore. At first I thought they were otters, seen rather frequently in the lakes. But otters cavort and play tag, disappearing and reappearing, poking up heads to look around now and then. This stolid pair was swimming steadily. I reached for the binoculars and saw they were beavers, heading for the shore about 200 feet across from our campsite. I handed the glasses to Dick and we took turns watching while they climbed out on the bank and moved around, snacking on willow branches. Magnified seven times, they appeared to be about 30 feet from us. I had the exciting feeling that these big, sleek animals were practically sitting in my lap!

There couldn't have been a more satisfying ending to our day but the treats weren't over yet. It must have been sometime after midnight that I came awake to what seemed a predawn light in the tent until I noticed leaf shadows on the ceiling. The illumination was coming from a full moon. I had a feeling that a sound had awakened me but I heard nothing. Not even small rustles of leaves or lapping of water disturbed the stillness. Then I heard it. From far off came a howl, thin and clear, a sad sound that rose and lowered, and ended on an upturn of voice like a sob. A second howl followed closely, another, fading away on a high note. Silence. Then a chorus of howls, rising and lowering, culminating in excited yapping. Wolves were singing!

I lay very still listening to the spine-tingling sounds until they died away for the last time. Dick seemed to be asleep.

In the morning he said he'd heard them too. How lucky can you get, we asked each other, gazing across the lake as we sipped our breakfast coffee on the rock overlook. Of three billion people in the world today how many do you suppose have heard the howl of a wolf pack in its natural habitat?

Before our trip was over we returned to Winchell Lake and camped there a few days, finding it as wildly beautiful and unpeopled as the previous year. A couple of parties paddled through from the portage out of Wanihigan Lake but the campsites remained unoccupied.

Paddling close to Winchell's southern shore on our return to Gaskin the last morning, we heard a roar of water ahead. It came from a stream deep in the woods cascading down over a tumble of rocks about 40 feet high. Dick nosed the canoe in to shore beside it.

"There could be a trail up there," he said, peering up into the tangle of rocks and brush. "This stream originates in Tremble Lake, a little lake about a quarter mile up over that ridge."

Finding no trace of a path of any sort, we shoved off again. As we moved slowly out into the big lake, we stopped and stared back at the awesome cliffs towering some 300 feet above us. A gleam of adventure shone in Dick's dark eyes as he turned to pick up his paddle again. "Some day I'm going to take a look around up there," he said.

It was a prediction he was to keep four years later.

In the meantime our summer trips took us to other areas of the BWCA. Once we set off from Ely down Fernberg Road, taking a two-rutted woods road to Snowbank, a large beautiful lake with interesting islands and bays but disappointing with its resorts and cottages. Another time we put in on Bearskin Lake, a short distance off the Gunflint Trail, and portaged over to Alder and Canoe Lakes. For some reason—perhaps because of raw September weather—we found the long stretches of paddling tiring, the lakes uninspiring, and soon returned.

The summer of 1972 found us exploring the Sawbill Lake area, conveniently reached by the Sawbill Trail from the little town of Tofte. On our first trip we took a unique portage with steel rails (on which you pushed your gear on a little open car) from Sawbill Lake to Alton. From there we portaged over to Beth. The lakes were all fairly large and attractive but people were everywhere and unoccupied campsites were hard to find. We were lucky to move into one on Beth as former occupants were leaving.

A popular vehicle campground and resorts have brought an influx of campers of all varieties to Sawbill. The whine of motors is heard everywhere on the lake and because of the "railway" portage, sizeable power boats are easily transported across to Alton too. On a couple of shorter trips we camped on a good rocky knoll on a small western inlet of Sawbill but even here small motors were frequent disturbers of the peace. One summer was enough; we never went back.

In 1973 the time seemed ripe for a return to the South Kawishiwi River. It was five years since our last visit and we were eager for a canoe trip in an area we liked.

We shoved off from the campground boat landing under blue skies one August morning with a week at our disposal. Our aim was to make a permanent camp in a wide lake-like place about 14 or 15 miles up the river where the South Kawishiwi separated from the Kawishiwi. We hoped to make an overnight stop along the way at the campsite we had enjoyed so much on previous trips.

A leak around a loose rivet in the stern soon changed our minds. It was trouble we'd had before in our aging canoe, which Dick had taken care of successfully with an epoxy glue. Apparently the rocky landings had opened up the leak again. So much bailing was becoming necessary to keep the packs dry we decided to pull in at a convenient campsite beside a portage landing to repair it. (Dick had wisely brought along some glue.) It would need overnight curing time.

The portage was at the foot of a wide stretch of shallow, rocky rapids about a quarter of a mile long. Steve and Pat had made a flawless run on their memorable trip together but other combinations in our party had hit at least one rock.

Avoiding rocks wasn't everybody's goal in running rapids, we were to find out while camping by the landing. We were eating lunch when shouts from young voices came from upstream. Aluminum whacking granite began to shatter the quiet. We hurried to the riverbank to see what was going on. A canoe came bumping its way down the rapids, colliding with rock after rock. Four or five others followed in this fashion, each boat loaded with two or three laughing teenagers.

"They should be able to steer around the rocks better than that," I said to Dick.

"They're not trying to steer around—they're aiming for them!" he said, shaking his head in disbelief.

The first boatloads began paddling back from the quiet

water below the rapids. At the same time a young couple emerged from the trail, the man portaging a canoe which he set down at the water's edge. They were the counselors for this church-camp group, we learned, striking up a conversation. They'd been up the river for a few days and were ending their trip today at the South Kawishiwi Campground.

Altogether there were 15 in their party. Two of their seven canoes had to be portaged and towed because of bad leaks, the man explained. The kids were pretty hard on them. With a resigned shrug he pointed at the bandaid and chewing gum patches on the craft he had just portaged.

By now the young canoeists were milling around on shore, chatting noisily, roughhousing, having a great time. The man shouted to one of the huskier boys to go over the portage for the other canoe. Lunches were dug out of packs. Kids sprawled on the rocks or dove off of them, yelling back and forth as they drifted downstream with the current. We'd lost track of the woman among the girls. Both counselors seemed little older than their charges.

Dick and I soon retreated the short distance to our campsite.

"Do you get the feeling you're camping in the middle of Grand Central Station?" I asked.

Dick nodded with a laugh. In a way it was fun. They were nice kids, if a bit exuberant—but the peace and quiet sure were great when they left.

We were sitting around a campfire late that evening, enjoying its warmth since the sun had gone down, when we were surprised to see a bearded young man in a wide-brimmed, flat-topped hat coming over a rise into our camp. He called a greeting and said he was camped farther down the riverbank—thought he'd come over to say hello.

The usual exchange of canoe country small talk, "How long you been out?" "Where you heading?" etc., developed into a fascinating evening's conversation. It turned out he was David Bixler, professor of ecology at Chaffey College in Alta Loma, California. His visit to the BWCA was part of a long term study of the role of the beaver in North America ecology. This summer he was making a survey in the east and earlier in the season had been in Labrador and Maine.

Participation in an environmental impact study of the proposed route of the Alaska pipeline had made him a strong opponent. His special concern was the caribou, whose migration route included a narrow pass through which the pipeline was to be built. It was the only way through that part of the Brooks Range for either caribou or man. When he had been there, before any construction had begun, vehicular traffic was already seriously interferring with their migration. We sometimes wonder, now that the pipeline is built, whether his dire predictions about wildlife have been borne out.

Before the evening was through we exchanged anecdotes about bears and opinions regarding wilderness travel. His choice was the kayak. For his one man expeditions he found this type of craft easier to handle and better protection for his professional photography equipment. As for rapids, he portaged every one to prevent damage from rocks to the fabric covering.

He too had witnessed the teenagers' hit or miss descent of the rapids that afternoon. He'd been exploring the opposite shore for signs of beaver habitat and had had a grandstand seat. "Sounded like dishpans in a bowling alley," was his description. All of us were grinning but expressed empathy for the outfitter who had rented the canoes.

By the time our interesting visitor had left the stars were out and our campfire had died to a few glowing coals.

In the morning Dick found the glue cured to satisfactory hardness. The day's trip began with portaging across the easy, well-trodden trail. Paddling on up the river, we passed the site we had camped at other years and found a tent pitched and gear on the picnic table. No boat at the shore edge meant the occupants were probably out fishing. At the campsite across the river we saw a couple of canoes pulled up on the rocks and the glint of sun on aluminum up the long beach ahead indicated two or three more. As we passed the boundary into BWCA territory we seemed to find canoeists around every bend and most campsites occupied. It was hard to believe this was the same area we'd had almost to ourselves five years ago. An even bigger surprise awaited us.

Paddling through narrows out into a wide, many-inleted basin where the last five or six mile stretch of the river turned north, we suddenly felt surrounded. Everywhere we looked the steep, rocky hillsides sprouted shorts-and-T-shirted young people— climbing, sitting, shouting back and forth. Canoes were pulled out any place a landing could be made. Others were still coming downriver. They all seemed to be one group, older than yesterday's teenagers and about twice as many.

"We might as well have gone camping in a public park!" I groaned.

"At least they're coming from where we're going. That must leave two or three empty campsites at the very least," Dick said optimistically.

It was depressing nonetheless. We had given up the Sea-gull Lake area because of a large increase in the number of canoe-ists and now it looked like the South Kawishiwi was heading in the same direction. Overcrowding in the BWCA was becoming a serious problem. Something would have to be done or the wilderness would be destroyed by those wanting most to enjoy it.

(In 1976 the Forest Service came up with a solution in the form of reservations. As of this writing, the plan has been in operation for three seasons and has worked very well, I understand. For details, see Appendix.)

Rounding a bend, we put the last of the canoeists behind us and headed for an inlet where a short portage skirted rapids. The sheltered cove was woodland quiet. As we slid silently to shore a dark form streaked from the shallows and melted into the brush bordering the stream. A mink? Overhead a loon called as it winged a straight course for wider reaches of the river. Dick nosed the canoe in gently and we sat watching it out of sight, savoring—if for the moment only—our private patch of wilderness.

Chapter 13
Ordeal at Tremble Lake

Principal Lakes: Winchell, Gaskin, Tremble

"I've got a great idea!" I said. "How about taking off the week of the Memorial Day holiday for a canoe trip?"

Dick shook his head. "Worst time of year—there's too many people."

"Not if we start the Monday everybody's coming back. Bet we'd have the wilderness all to ourselves the rest of the week."

"Well. . . maybe you've got something there. Fishing season opens the weekend before so that mad rush would be over."

"And the weather should be perfect—warm enough to camp but too cold for bugs."

This discussion was taking place on a raw Sunday in March. Not a hint of spring was in the air, but we looked out at snowdrifts and gray skies and saw blue lakes under a smiling summer's sun. It didn't take long to make a decision. The last week in May would open the season for our canoe trips this year.

Dick had an added inspiration. "Hey, see if you can talk Pat and Curt into coming with us!"

"Terrific! I'll do my best," I promised.

Our daughter Pat was now married and living in Cambridge, Massachusetts and I was looking forward to a visit next month. Pat's husband, Curt, was a boat enthusiast friend of our son Dicky. Most of Pat and Curt's first dates had taken place on a catamaran in Boston Harbor.

Their present interests included outdoors and wild places. Tied to city jobs, they escaped on weekends and vacations to hike the woods and mountains of New Hampshire and Maine, as well as sail the coasts. Pat had never forgotten her BWCA canoe trip with us in college years and had been pushing the idea with Curt for a vacation there.

CANOEING THE BOUNDARY WATERS

The timing was right and before I left Boston in April plans were made for their visit with us the last week in May.

Dick and I decided on Winchell Lake as a good location for a base camp with interesting possibilities for side trips. I wrote ahead to reserve a canoe from Carl Brandt, proprietor of the Nor-'wester on Poplar Lake, from whom we'd rented Steve and Mike's canoe. Pat and Curt would bring their packs, tent and backpacking gear with them.

We picked them up at the Minneapolis airport the Friday evening before the holiday. On Sunday we drove to Grand Marais, spending the night in a rented cabin to allow an early morning start on the lakes.

We couldn't have asked for better weather that Monday—crisp, cool air with a warming sun. By the time we'd covered the distance across Poplar Lake jackets were coming off. Curt guided their canoe into the portage landing, unloaded, and swung it up on his shoulders with ease. Tall and slim, an expert in karate and a teacher of the skill, his six-foot-two frame was well muscled.

As we had expected, traffic coming from the opposite direction began getting heavy. There were lineups at the portage landings and we were frequently stepping to the side on trails to allow others to pass. I was also burdened with a dog on a leash. Once again we had our pup with us, this time a small schnauzer named Fritz, replacement for Tuffy who had died in an accident a few years before. With so many people I felt I should keep him restrained. By the time we reached Gaskin Lake we'd had enough. There was no problem finding vacated campsites. We moved into one on top of a heavily wooded slope. By late afternoon we were glad of the tree cover as our fine day had rapidly disintegrated and rain was coming down.

In the morning the rain had stopped and we set forth on a misty gray lake to explore the many inlets, bays and islands at the western end. The wilderness was all ours now and Fritz had a great time exploring trails and wild animal paths every time we stopped.

With only a short distance to go for the day's travel, we struck a leisurely pace after lunch. It took us awhile to get over the steep portage into Winchell with the young people making extra trips. For once I wasn't carrying my share. Some minor back pains had sent me to a doctor during the winter and a chronic disc problem was discovered. I had received orders not to lift or carry anything heavy. Furthermore, every precaution should be taken to prevent a fall, as it could result in hospitalization. It was enough to keep me cautious.

Pat and Curt, paddling ahead down Winchell, came upon our former campsite first and were enthusiastic about its jutting rock peninsula and hilly terrain. It didn't take long for the four of us to set up camp and get a supper fire going. By now the sun had broken through thinning clouds and the evening was clear and beautiful. Seated on rocks facing the western end of the lake, we were treated to a flamboyant sunset in hot pinks.

We took our time getting off in the morning on a day trip. Heading into a brisk wind, we set a northerly course for a portage over to Omega Lake where we paddled deep, quiet bays and climbed out on a sunny slope to eat lunch. Then, continuing on north, we stroked down a long inlet from the end of which a couple of portages with a puddle-sized lake between led to a remote lake called Finn. The portage turned out to be badly overgrown. Our pup enjoyed it tremendously but after scrambling over boulders, slippery rocks and mud holes for a while, Dick and I decided to turn back. The risk of a fall seemed a little too high for comfort.

Later, seated on logs around the campfire, Curt and Pat told us about Finn Lake.

"It's really wild and beautiful," Pat said. "It didn't look like anyone had ever been there. We paddled its length and there was no sign of a campsite."

Curt nodded. "I don't think a tent had ever been pitched or a fire built anywhere. There was a little point we thought of camping on but didn't want to spoil it."

Pat explained they'd been thinking about an overnight side trip before we started back in a couple of days—how did we feel about it? We thought it a great idea and brought out maps to help them plan. Before we turned in that night they had decided upon a circle of lakes through Wanihigan, Cliff, North Cone, Davis and Pup.

It was nearly noon before they got off, saying they'd return the afternoon of the following day. Plans are best kept flexible in canoe country but they'd at least be back in time for supper the next night, they promised.

Clouds that had been gathering soon blanketed the sky. We'd hardly had a day without some rain and, true to form, a downpour sent us into our tent early that night. In the morning the sun awakened us and we ate an early breakfast under a cloudless sky. Two loons dove for fish in the rippled lake while on the shore opposite our cove a great blue heron stalked unwary prey in the shallows with slow, measured strides.

By 8 o'clock the gentle westerly breeze had gained

strength, stirring up choppy waves. Dick had been quietly studying the map while I cleaned up breakfast dishes and I sensed something was afoot. Finally he voiced his thoughts.

"I've been thinking about Tremble Lake—you know, that
little lake up over the ridge on the opposite shore where that
stream was coming from," he said, hesitating.

I nodded, guessing what was coming.

"Would you mind if I took a hike up there this morning?
I probably won't be gone more than an hour or two and we can
go out for a paddle when I get back."

I didn't mind a bit. I had a few clothes to wash out and
I always enjoyed a campsite to myself for awhile. Besides, I had
Fritz for company. However, it did worry me to have him go off
so far alone. I started to protest, then changed my mind. Why be
a spoilsport? My fears usually turned out to be groundless. It
was okay with me, I said, but he better make sure he had a compass. Right here in my pocket, he showed me.

Shortly after eight he shoved the canoe into the lake, re-
fusing my offer of a candy bar or sandwich.

"Don't need it. I'll be back in time for an early lunch,"
he said, pushing out from shore with strong strokes.

"Well, it's been a good 40 years!" I called after him,
laughing, wanting to give him a lighthearted send-off. (Just the
day before we'd talked about our upcoming 36th wedding anniversary and how we'd known each other for exactly 40 years.)

I doubt he even heard me. Eyes raised to the cliffs on the
opposite shore, he was already in another world, climbing to the
little hidden lake.

Fritz and I went back up the path. For an hour or so I
busied myself with camp chores, then settled in a comfortable spot
with the book I'd brought along. When three hours had gone by I
told myself he was having fun and had lost track of time. I had
discovered his watch in the tent so it wasn't surprising.

Not until noon did I really begin to worry. He didn't
need a watch to tell him he was hungry, and by now he'd be
ravenous. Something had gone wrong. With a compass and the
sun I couldn't believe he was lost. Had he fallen and injured himself? Whatever the trouble, I had no way to go looking for him. I
went back down to the shore he had left from to scan the lake to
the east. There was no sign of a canoe. Returning to the campfire,
I stirred up the coals of a dwindling fire and added sticks to send
up a blaze under the pot of pea soup I'd made earlier.

By 1 o'clock I had sipped a small cup of soup, covered the pot, and let the fire die down. It was too early to expect Pat and Curt but I hiked out to the tip of the peninsula, the dog at my heels, and trained the binoculars on the far west end of the lake where they'd be emerging from a portage. Every few minutes I glanced back eastward, hoping to see Dick paddling around the point. Fritz, sensitive to my mood, pressed close to my legs when I settled on a rock.

Since noon the wind had risen alarmingly and now my worries took a new direction. A choppy lake sparkling in the sunlight had become a seething dark blue sea with long white-capped waves rolling in to break over the rocks in showers of spray. How easy it would be for a person alone in a lightweight boat to be swept broadside to the waves. It would swamp in seconds. Dick could be anywhere in the lake clinging to the canoe—providing he could hang on in high waves and numbing cold water! I shut the picture out of my mind and concentrated on where I knew the portage entrance must be.

It seemed hours later, though actually not much after 2 o'clock, when I first saw the dark dot at the end of the lake. Gradually it took on the shape of a canoe. It had to be Curt and Pat! (Since the first day of our trip we had seen only one other boat, at a distance on another lake.) I jumped to my feet, laughing and crying with relief, the little dog leaping and barking beside me.

Perched on a rock at the farthest edge of the peninsula, I watched the progress of the oncoming canoe through the binoculars. As it reached the widest, roughest stretch of lake I saw they were close to trouble in the cresting waves. Driven by the wind and rollers, they hurtled forward. Paddling fast was the only way to keep control of the canoe. Finally they made it okay and headed in for a landing in the sheltered cove. Concern grew on Pat's face as they came close. She must have noticed our canoe missing from its usual beached spot.

"Where's Daddy?" she called out anxiously.

"He's gone. . . " My resolve to give a calm account of events fell apart. "Since. . early. . morning," I sobbed.

"Don't worry about Dick," Curt said quickly. "He's holed up on shore somewhere waiting out the blow. He's too good a canoeist to risk paddling alone into this wind."

Of course he was right—why hadn't I thought of that!

"The wind will probably drop around four. If he hasn't come back by then, we'll go looking for him," he assured me.

The two were hungry as bears, not having stopped for lunch. While Pat and I got busy preparing a meal Curt unpacked and set up their tent. What sweet relief to get my mind on other things! Pat filled me in on details of their trip as we worked. They had especially liked Davis Lake, where they'd camped—it hardly had any signs of use, she said. Later she told me how they had planned to spend the morning exploring it, but she had awakened with a strange urgency to get back and had insisted on leaving right away.

They scarcely finished eating when the sky darkened and to our amazement, pea-sized hailstones started falling. We ran for shelter in our tents. Where was Dick, I wondered—it was getting harder to believe he was all right.

By 4 o'clock the wind had slackened but there was still no sign of Dick. Pat and I were growing anxious. Curt gathered up map, compass and a hearty snack for Dick and shoved their canoe in the water. I pointed out Tremble Lake and the stream on their map and they set off. Concerned that I might fall climbing the rough terrain up the ridge, they had persuaded me to remain on the campsite. They could cover ground faster alone too.

I watched until the canoe disappeared around the bend, grateful for my little canine companion at my side. Worries that had been pushed to the back of my mind now came crowding back. Curt had been sure Dick would not try to paddle alone into the gale force wind but what if he had started out from shore before he realized how strong it was? Once out in those waves it would have been impossible to turn back without swamping. The more I thought about it, the more convinced I became that that was what had happened. They would find him somewhere in the lake clinging to the canoe, exhausted. Or would they find only the empty canoe? My last words to Dick that morning came back to stab me—"It's been a good 40 years!" Had it been a premonition?

The lightweight craft could have blown down the length of the lake by now. It might be a long time before the young folks came back. Unable to sit still, I paced the campsite—up to the tent, down to the campfire, and out on the rocks to peer as far east as I could see down the empty lake. Then back again, over and over, Fritz at my heels or trotting ahead with frequent backward glances to make sure I was coming. I began to know every rock and ridge, and almost every pebble, by heart. I could have walked the route blindfolded.

It was some time around 7 o'clock that I heard voices. Racing to the lake edge with the best view to the east, I finally saw Curt and Pat rounding the far point. As far as I could tell they were alone. Then I saw that they were towing an empty canoe!

Over my rising panic I could just make out Pat's shouting. "We found him! He's okay."

He wasn't exactly okay, I learned as soon as they got to shore, but Pat had guessed my reaction to the towed canoe and had been anxious to allay my worst fears.

They had found him near the little lake, pinned under a boulder that had fallen during a rockslide.

"It took a long time to get him free, Mother, but he seems all right, except for his right leg. He can't walk."

Horrifying pictures were forming in my mind.

"It's not too bad," Curt broke in. "There's a deep gash on his knee I cleaned up, and he can't bear weight on that leg. It may be broken." He started up the path to the tent, calling over his shoulder. "No time to talk. I want to get back to him before it gets dark. You two pack food and warm clothes while I get a tarp and sleeping bags. I'm taking our backpack stove too."

Pat explained their plan as we got things together. Curt was returning to stay with her father tonight; she would be here with me. In the morning he would paddle back to the outfitter's where we'd started off. A float plane was needed to get Dick out.

Curt was striding down the path, cramming gear into his pack. "Don't forget to have breakfast ready as soon as it's light."

Throwing his pack into the canoe, he leaped in after it and paddled off with long, deep strokes. I still felt bewildered and upset about what had happened to Dick but greatly relieved and thankful for my son-in-law's competence and calm authority.

Pat filled me in on the rest of the story that evening. They had discovered Dick's canoe pulled up on shore near the stream I'd pointed out on the map and had climbed up beside it over rocks, blowdowns and through thick brush. All the while they kept calling and finally, when Tremble Lake came into view, they thought they heard a faint answer. More calls brought another answer. Eventually they were led to him in this fashion.

"We might never have found him, Mother, if he hadn't been able to call," Pat said. "He was in a dark hollow at the base of a cliff a distance back from the lake edge. Trees and dense vegetation hid him from view until we were almost on him."

He had been on his way back to the campsite, he had told them, using his compass to take a shorter route over the cliffs. Climbing up, he had disturbed a big rock that had started a rockslide. This had nudged the boulder that toppled on him. It pinned him face down with his right leg bent back. Wedged against the protruding root of a large pine, he couldn't move and had lain there six or seven hours. "Curt figured the rock must have weighed at least 400 pounds," Pat said.

"How did you ever get it off of him?" I gasped.

"That's what took us so long. There was nothing to use as a lever—we hadn't taken along a hatchet. Finally Curt worked out a way of raising a corner of the boulder an inch or two at a time by wedging small rocks under it. I searched for rocks and pushed them in while Curt lifted. The big rock was sort of box shaped and we had to do this to all four courners several times before we got it high enough. Then Curt held it while I helped pull Daddy out. At first he felt so good we were sure we could bring him back with us but finally we had to give up. Every way we tried it hurt him too much to walk and Curt was afraid he'd injure him more if he tried carrying him over such rough terrain."

I was near tears and felt sick thinking about it. Pat tried to reassure me. "His spirits are good, Mother. He was talking with us and helping direct his rescue."

We both knew his indelible optimism and take-life-as-it-comes attitude would do a lot to see him through and it was comforting knowing Curt was with him. Nevertheless, we spent a restless night. As soon as it was light enough to see we were up gathering wood for the fire, thankful that it looked like the weather was holding good. By the time Curt's canoe slid in through the morning mists we had an omlet and coffee ready.

"He slept fairly well but he's weak," he answered our anxious questions. "He can't stay alone. I'm taking Pat back to be with him before I leave."

While Curt was eating I got together soup and cocoa packets, dried fruit and candy bars, and made cheese sandwiches for Pat to take with her, as well as some for Curt.

"Will this be enough for Dick?" I asked.

Curt looked somber. "He doesn't want anything to eat. Water, a little cocoa and a piece of bread were all he'd take last night. Nothing but water this morning."

I stared at him in shock. No matter what happened Dick always ate. I'd known only a few occasions, when he was really sick, that he didn't have a good appetite. For the first time I understood what bad shape he was in.

Once again, Fritz at my feet, I watched as Pat and Curt paddled swiftly away. They had argued against my pleas to go along, pointing out that they might have to carry two out on stretchers if I tried it.

"I should have a plane in here by noon," Curt called over his shoulder.

Knowing that Pat was with her father and that help was on its way made waiting a little easier this time. It was good to busy myself with camp cleanup and packing for the return trip. We would start back as soon as Dick was flown out to the Grand Marais hospital.

By 11 o'clock, although I knew it was too soon, I began listening for the sound of an airplane. Three or four times after the noon hour came I ran down to the rocks, thinking I heard one. Fritz raced ahead, leaping and barking in response to my excitement. My mind was constantly on Dick and Pat now. In what condition had she found him? Was he in pain? Could she get him to eat? . . . Oh, God, where was the plane? I took a dry sandwich down to the shore nearest Tremble Lake and nibbled it sitting on a rock facing the ridge. It was only about a mile as the crow flies from where Dick lay and helped me feel closer.

Around 2 o'clock the sound of an aircraft was unmistakable. Soon it appeared over the trees. Flying low, it circled and then dropped behind the horizon, landing on the little lake, I assumed. In spite of the relief I found myself tense and near tears. My eyes riveted to the hills where I'd last seen the plane, I waited impatiently for its reappearance. An hour crept by. Then another. What was taking so long? The worst ordeal of waiting during the whole two days took place those last hours.

Finally, a little before 4 o'clock, the plane soared up over the tree line and headed in the direction of Grand Marais. To my great surprise and relief within minutes Curt and Pat paddled into view. I had been prepared for a long wait while they made their way down the ledge.

"Daddy's okay," Pat assured me when they came into shore. "Tremble Lake was too small to land on so the pilot had to set down on Winchell." (It was around the bend from me so I had neither seen nor heard it.)

Carl Brandt, the outfitter, had come with them and all three men had climbed the ledge to bring Dick down on a stretcher, they told me. Carrying him over the half mile of dense brush, boulders and fallen trees had been a long, difficult undertaking. It was lucky Brandt was with them. A Paul Bunyan of a man and native of the area, he was well acquainted with trail breaking. A sequence was developed in which Brandt went ahead 50 yards or so clearing brush, then returned to help carry the stretcher to the end of the cleared place. Pat followed with the gear. This procedure was repeated many times before they reached the plane.

Curt said he had made it back to the outfitter's well before noon but the two hour delay had been caused because government "red tape" or something had prevented the Forest Service from sending their plane. Time was lost finding a pilot who was willing to leave immediately on the rescue mission and in getting permission to fly into the BWCA (from which private aircraft are excluded to preserve the atmosphere of the wilderness). Brandt had called several pilots before locating Dale Chilson, proprietor of Gunflint Canada Airways.

"The pilot's coming back for you," Curt told me now. "He's going to fly you and Fritz and the gear back to Poplar Lake where we left the car so you can get to the hospital. Pat and I will paddle out tonight—without packs we can make it easily. Brandt has promised us a cabin to sleep in, then you can come pick us up tomorrow."

By the time I got to the hospital Dick had been made as comfortable as possible but it was still painful for him to move at all. In spite of his wan and weary appearance, he was in his usual good spirits. The doctor's report was both good and bad. The best news was that he hadn't gone into shock, which had quite amazed the medical staff and would greatly help in his recovery. X-rays had shown a fractured sacrum. The right leg appeared to have been dislocated at the hip joint but had slipped back by itself. A deep knee cut required an anesthetic to be cleaned but was too swollen for stitches at this point. Only time would tell if numbness in his right foot would disappear. He'll probably be on crutches for the first six months or so. There's a possibility he may never walk again, the doctor told me.

Dick's worst problem turned out to be dehydration. After two days on intravenous drip a serious kidney disorder developed and he was transferred to a Duluth hospital. Luckily the condition began to clear up without the need of a dialysis machine. In another week or so he was transferred down to our local hospital where our family doctor encouraged him to get out of bed and start using a walker. By now the numbness in his foot was pretty well gone. That seemed to be all Dick was waiting for.

"I'll be walking okay again before you know it," he said, practicing every day up and down the corridors. He also went at his physical therapy sessions like he was going out for a sport.

Altogether he spent three weeks in hospitals. Before he

was discharged the final time he had traded his walker for a cane. At home less than an hour and he was on his way up to his office about 500 feet away. (Dick has his own research and development business in a small laboratory across the road.) By the time he came back he had discarded the cane and never used it again. Eventually all his problems cleared up and at present, three and a half years later, he's in excellent health.

Whenever people heard the details of Dick's accident they almost always asked about the six or seven hours he spent trapped under the rock. How did he endure it? What were his thoughts? Why had he gone off alone in a trailless wilderness? While in the hospital he spent some time writing his own account of the happenings, which answers these questions. His story follows.

Chapter 14
To Be In a Wild Place

(By Dick Stresau)

The whole cliff seemed to be coming out at me. I tried to leap clear but a boulder, nudged by sliding rocks, toppled over on my back, forcing me face down and catching my legs as in a vise. My right leg, doubled back in a cramped position, was wedged between the boulder and a protruding root of a large pine tree, trapping me. A few experimental squirms and wiggles made it clear that the rock pinning my legs was too heavy to escape.

My first reaction was, pointlessly, a somewhat profane self-recrimination for getting myself into such a jam. There was no way to summon help. That someone else might be poking around this off-trail bit of wilderness at the same time was too remote a possibility for more than a passing thought. Rescue by Curt and Pat was my only reasonable hope—but that would be afternoon.

I struggled more vigorously to free myself, thinking of the worry I'd be causing Emmy and the trouble for others. All I succeded in doing was wiggling the rock a bit and causing the pain in my leg to increase. I'd have to resign myself to waiting. Having forgotten my watch, I could only guess at the time but the position of the sun seemed to indicate 10 or 11 o'clock. That made it two or three hours at the very earliest before Curt and Pat could be expected. Four or five would be more realistic.

There was, of course, a possibility that something might delay their return to the campsite. I also had to face the fact that I might not be found at all. I had fallen into a shadowy pocket of trees and rocks a hundred yards or so from the stream. Should I drift into sleep or unconsciousness my dark clothes would make me almost impossible to spot. I thought about that a while and came to the conclusion that at least I couldn't imagine a more beautiful place to die. But, in truth, I never really seriously doubted that I'd be found.

The only sensible thing to do was make myself as comfortable as possible. I was hanging with my head downhill, my thighs clamped about midpoint between the rock and tree root, with no support for my torso except my arms. I found I could support myself "push up" fashion on a ledge about a foot below. When my arms grew tired I relaxed forward but this increased the painful contact between my thighs and the root. I tried to build up a mound of whatever I could reach, small rocks, moss, mud, sticks, high enough to support my chest. It was hard to scrape together enough loose material. After working an hour or so I managed to pile up a mound high enough to provide some support, but never quite enough. Fairly frequent changes between the alternate positions resulted in the least discomfort.

Now and then I tried, by wiggling the rock, to improve the circulation in my right foot, which had "gone to sleep." This didn't help. The foot soon became completely numb. Remembering my Boy Scout first aid training about loosening tourniquets every 20 minutes, I had some worrisome thoughts about gangrene.

Before the accident happened I had been admiring the blue gem of a lake nestled beneath red cliffs and tall dark pines, enjoying my wild surroundings. The primitive little lake was as beautiful as before. Downhill, through the openings between foliage and tree trunks, some a yard thick, blue patches of water sparkled as the ripples caught the sun. The wind still sighed through the pine boughs, birds discussed their daily business, and in the distance the shallow stream burbled over the rocks. In spite of my situation and discomfort I continued to appreciate the unspoiled beauty. Though, I had to admit, my exclusive possession of it had lost some of its attractiveness.

People often ask how I passed the time. Mainly I tried to keep my mind occupied. For a while I turned my thoughts to my business, the scheduling of projects, profit and loss prospects and personnel questions. Sometimes I attempted to solve mathematical problems but without paper and pencil didn't accomplish much.

Once I amused myself for some time with a piece of "foxfire" wood I had come upon in the course of digging the mound. It was a twig about the size of a pencil, which glowed a rich iridescent green at the broken ends. I shaded it with my hands to make it dark enough to see the glow, finally breaking off a few piec and shoving them in my jacket pocket to keep as souvenirs. They must have fallen out as I never did find them later.

It was hard to keep my mind off both the physical discomfort and the stupidity of my situation. Unfortunately, I couldn't seem to keep myself from occasionally trying to squirm free. A little progress resulted but my clothes caught and twisted, exposing my back. The new positions were always less comfortable than the previous ones.

Even in May the BWCA has its share of insect life, including a variety of species which attack humans. At one time a couple of horseflies buzzed around, making me a bit nervous. But eventually they ignored me, flying over to sit on a log and do their own thing.

The progress of the sun, now past its zenith, indicated that a couple of hours or more had passed. I was getting thirsty, a condition reinforced by the steady drip of what looked like crystal clear water a few inches beyond my reach. A short time later what I could see of the sky grew dark and a brief hailstorm provided a few not entirely unpleasant twinges to my bare midriff. I picked up what hailstones I could reach (about the size of peas) and tried to quench my thirst but my hands were so muddy they did more harm than good.

Soon after this I heard noises which could be interpreted as the results of human scrambling over the rough terrain. Perhaps it wasn't too early to expect Pat and Curt—or maybe someone else.

"Help me! Anybody. I need help!" I called out.

The only answer was woodland noises.

On the sheltered shore of the small lake I had no way of knowing of the gale force winds on Winchell. Curt and Pat could be on their way now, I figured. They'd probably come alone. My wife's back problem would make it too risky for her. I began calling frequently but stopped after a while, the dryness of my mouth making me afraid of losing my voice. Time stretched out and I began contemplating the possibility of spending the night under the rock. I wondered what would happen to my right foot.

I'm not sure how long after that a different sound began to penetrate my consciousness. Mixed with the bird calls and wind in the trees it seemed at first my imagination. Then unmistakably it was Pat's voice. I answered each call but she apparently didn't hear. After a while her calls became fainter, seeming to fade in the distance. Were they looking on the wrong side of Tremble Lake?

In a few minutes the calls got stronger again. Then Pat heard my answer; she asked where I was. I heard Curt's voice too and tried to give my location. They didn't seem to understand so I just kept calling, hoping they could locate me by the sound.

Soon Pat appeared from behind a rock about 20 feet away. When she saw me she cried out, "Oh, Daddy!" and broke into tears.

Curt took hold of her. "Cut that out, Pat!" he said firmly.

He spent a few minutes helping her pull herself together, pointing out that she wouldn't be much help in that condition, then lost no time surveying my situation and arriving at a general plan of action.

The rock was too large to lift in one motion. The use of logs as levers was considered and rejected because Curt had doubts he could control the rock well enough to avoid injuring me further. In any case, fallen logs and dead trees nearby were rotten and unusable. The method finally adopted was to lift an edge or corner of the rock an inch or two, wedge a small rock under it, then repeat this operation at another corner. Pat kept busy fetching rocks and inserting them while Curt lifted.

At one point I asked the time and was told 5 o'clock. Unaccountably I was surprised to hear it was that late.

As the process progressed, strains were released and I became more comfortable. Finally all pressures were relieved and I could move but when I tried to pull myself out, my feet acted as hooks, anchoring me. The far end of the rock had to be lifted and wedged higher. This shifted its weight so that most of it now bore on my rump. For a moment or two the pressure brought pain greater than I'd felt all day. Then, somehow, Curt lifted the near end of the rock and, with Pat's help, I pulled myself out.

Freed from the strain they'd been under for so many hours, my legs felt so good I was sure I was ready to walk out. I rested while Curt cleaned and dressed a nasty gash on my right knee. Then they helped me to my feet. I took a step and a half before my right leg collapsed with sharp pains at knee and hip. Various positions and techniques were tried to help me walk but none would work in the dense brush. It was now 6:30 and the sun would set early behind the surrounding steep hills. Curt found a spot downhill which was reasonably flat and I slid and crawled to it crab fashion.

"We'll go back to camp and I'll return with sleeping bags, food and gear to spend the night," he said.

Pat was near tears again. "We can't leave Daddy here alone!" she protested.

"It's the only thing to do. Your mother doesn't know what's happened and she'll need you to stay with her," Curt told her. "Come on, let's get going. There's not much daylight left."

Assessing my apparent condition while they were gone, I found numerous gashes and bruises on my legs and one sizable lump where the rock had pinned them. My right foot was still numb and something was wrong with my right leg and hip. In some positions all pain could be eliminated but not for long. Soon my back, hip or knee would begin to hurt. Waiting for Curt's return, I found the time dragged more than it had all day. The sun sank below the hills and it grew cold. In spite of his jacket he had left me, I shivered violently from time to time.

It was nearly dark when he returned. He lost no time tying a tarp to trees to form a shelter and putting water to boil on his backpacking stove. He had brought the makings of a quick nourishing meal but all I wanted was a cup of cocoa and a piece of bread. With his help I got into my sleeping bag and slept most of the night. In the morning I couldn't move without pain. Curt had already made plans to bring Pat back to stay with me while he paddled to the outfitter's for help. A plane would be needed to get me out.

In spite of my discomfort the morning passed rather pleasantly after Pat arrived. It was good to have her company though I hated to be such a nuisance. She was constantly busy wedging rolled up jackets and sleeping bags under me to help relieve the pain each time I moved. She fetched water from the lake and was always encouraging me to eat. But for once in my life I had no appetite. What remains strongest in my memory of that morning is the time we had to talk and get to know each other better than we had in years. There was a closeness shared that probably could never have come about any other way.

By noon we started listening for planes. Once we heard one in the distance. Its sound increased, then faded. Minutes stretched out; then an hour. Finally, at almost 2 o'clock, the sound of an aircraft kept getting stronger until it appeared over the cliff. Pat grabbed an aluminum foil wrapper and dashed down to the lake edge, waving it in the bright sun. I could hear her sobbing when the plane went on down the lake. Then it doubled back. The pilot dipped his wings as he came near, apparently having seen her signal. But the plane continued on, disappearing over the cliffs and leaving us in silence again.

"This little lake is too small for a landing. They'll probably put down on Winchell," I told Pat.

In a half hour or so we heard a party coming through the woods. Curt appeared with Carl Brandt, the outfitter on Poplar Lake, and Dale Chilson, the pilot. They had brought a stretcher with them but getting me out wasn't all that simple. It took more than two hours of grueling work to travel the half mile to the plane. I was then transported swiftly to an airport on Devil's Track Lake, where an ambulance was waiting to rush me to Grand Marais hospital. Having been informed ahead concerning the nature of my accident, the doctors and nurses had been prepared for the worst. They were amazed to find how well I'd come through the ordeal.

People tell me they hope I've learned my lesson about

going off alone in the wilderness. Frankly, I haven't. To be in a wild place with no other human to break its spell is a need I have felt and satisfied from time to time as long as I can remember. I'm sure it will return.

One lesson I have learned, however, is to leave the cliffs alone in this area. The glaciers that formed this unique part of the country have only retreated about 10,000 years ago, leaving formations that are quite young compared to similar cliffs in other areas, which have been standing millions or even billions of years. This, plus the brittleness of the rocks and the action of the frost, which opens new cracks each year, makes the BWCA particularly dangerous for rock climbing. At least that's the way I see it.

The experience was, of course, one I'd never want to repeat. However, even the worst situation has its bright aspects. For me the combination of concern, kindness and exceptional effort on my behalf by so many has done much to reinforce my belief in the essential goodness of the human race.

Epilog

Dick and I haven't taken a canoe trip since the accident but we've been continuing to enjoy the northern lake country. In 1975 we acquired a camper and part of our vacations every summer are spent in the Superior National Forest campgrounds, from which we take day trips on nearby lakes and portages. Although we feel as eager and physically able to manage a canoe trip as we did ten years ago, we're a bit wary about being off very far alone in case a back problem should arise.

Last year when we were visiting Pat and Curt the subject of BWCA trips came up and the discussion grew lively talking about a future one. If they can work out a visit our way, we'll all go on another, it was decided.

"You sure you want to take a chance with us?" I laughed.

"You always take a chance when you go into the wilderness," Curt said. "What happened to Dick could have happened to me, or anyone."

"I don't know. Lots of people feel it's too risky going off alone, that he had no right to do it," I said.

"It's everyone's right to take a chance— a matter of choice," Curt insisted.

"To explore uninhabited wild places has been an American right from the start," Dick added. "Preserved wildernesses are all that are left of frontiers in the lower forty-eight states now."

"That's the main reason for preserving the BWCA as a completely wild area, as I see it," I put in. "Even when I get too old to enjoy it first hand, just knowing the wilderness is there and that others are paddling its lakes and climbing its portage trails will be enough to keep me happy."

Appendix
The Way to Go

If you are planning a canoe trip in the Boundary Waters Canoe Area and have never been there before, the first thing to do is write: Forest Supervisor, P. O. Box 338, Duluth MN 55801.

Ask for information on reservations for your trip. There is no charge but reservations and a permit are required for any overnight trip. A map of the BWCA entrance points (included here on page iv) and an explanation of the reservation system will be sent to you. (Reservations are necessary from mid-May through Labor Day and may be made starting January 1 each year.) Also ask them to include their brochures "The Boundary Waters Canoe Area" and "So You're Going to the BWCA." Everything you need to know for the trip is within the pages of these two booklets under headings: Equipment, Clothing, Food, Campsites, Fishing and Maps. Lakes and routes where motor powered watercraft may be used are listed (all other lakes are paddle-only). They even give you an interesting history of the geology of the area and a section on tree identification.

While the Forest Service brochures supply the essentials of how to take a BWCA canoe trip, a really good trip depends upon much more than that. In the course of our years of canoeing these wilderness lakes Dick and I worked out our own lists of what to take and what to leave at home, and gradually we acquired ways of doing things that have made the trips more fun.

In my opinion the first essential of trip planning is a list. We use three, in these categories: general supplies, food, and clothing. (If you're lucky enough to have access to a copying machine, you can make up a batch of copies of each, using a fresh sheet to check each trip.) The Forest Service booklet includes a general equipment list but you'll want to add your own personal choice items. Everyone's will be different. For instance, Dick and I consider the extra weight of a couple books, preferably paperback, and a camera well worth it. Others leave these behind but take fishing tackle, or a camp stove—or even an aluminum chaise lounge! Our choice of essentials and our way of doing things will probably not be yours but, for what they're worth, we pass on our "helpful hints."

GENERAL SUPPLY LIST

Binoculars — Although the Forest Service apparently does. not consider these a necessity, we do. Without them you'll have a much harder time finding portage entrances, campsites and whatever else you're trying to set a course for when paddling.

Fisher Maps — Most commonly used in BWCA travel. They are waterproof and are kept up to date with marked campsites and portage trail lengths included. They're available at most outfitters and resorts in the area or you can write to W. A. Fisher Co., Virginia MN 55792. Make sure you get the current year's edition for the most accurate campsite locations.

U.S. Geological Survey Maps — We learned the hard way never to take a canoe trip in a new area without them. They are topographical maps on a large scale with much detail not shown on Fisher maps. Some outfitters have them, or they may be purchased from: Denver Distribution Center, U.S. Geological Survey, Denver Federal Center, Building 41, Denver CO 80225.

Compass — A pocket compass is a necessity for off trail walks. Most campers use such a compass on the floor of their canoe to navigate, but it can slip out of view in rough weather. Dick solved the problem by fastening a bracket-mounted compass (the same kind used in cars) to the rear thwart of the canoe with a hose clamp.

Rope — We found that 1/8-inch nylon cord was the best size, useful for tents, tarps, bow rope on your canoe, and almost anything you need a rope for—except the food pack. You usually need something heavier to haul this up in a tree. A larger size nylon cord could be used, but Dick always took along a 50-foot length of 3/8-inch Manila rope because it didn't catch as easily in crotches of trees. Our advice is to take more rope (1/8-inch nylon) than you can imagine needing. For some reason you always find a use for it and it's easy and lightweight to pack.

Space Blanket — Only weighs 11 ounces but, as well as serving as a warm blanket, can be used as an effective insulator under your mattress if the ground is cold.

Matches — Wooden and waterproofed, the Forest Service suggests. We agree and add that a small plastic or metal container to keep them in near the fire grate is handy. We used to use a little screw-topped bottle but all bottles are now outlawed.

Aluminum Foil — Allowed, but you must carry every piece and scrap back out. If messy, seal in a plastic bag and throw away when you get home. If you take the heavy duty kind, an oven can be constructed from it (described in Chapter 2), which works very well. Later we acquired a camp oven, sold in most camping equipment stores or from catalogues. It's dandy, but if you're interested in cutting weight we recommend the former.

Paper Towels — These can be used for napkins, handkerchiefs, dish towels, even toilet paper if you run out. We used them to wipe out frying pans, pots, etc., if we were in a hurry to get off in the morning. Soap and water can come later. Buy two small-sized rolls instead of one big one, then squash each flat—they pack a lot easier. By the way, we notice the Forest Service does not have toilet paper on its lists of essentials and can't imagine why. Don't expect to find it hanging on the trees—bring your own!

Bath Towels — We took along two of the oldest, thinnest we could find at home and washed them out as needed. Spread over a pack or canoe thwart in the sun while traveling, they can even be dried en route.

Sewing Kit — Inside my zippered personal kit of comb, toothbrush, toothpaste, etc., I always tucked a small plastic change purse with different-sized needles, thread, thimble and tiny sicissors. It was useful when a strategic button came off, a seam ripped, or once for mending a torn pack. Include a few shirt-size buttons.

Plastic Wash Basin — I almost left this off the list, ashamed we toted such a civilized item, but it served many uses and fit easily into a pack. Stuffed with towels and small items, it took up very little space.

Five Quart Plastic Pail (with lid and handle) — An important piece of our equipment. We stowed it in the bow when paddling the lakes and carried it over the portages (usually filled with lunch, sun glasses, bug spray and small items). Kept handy; it can be used to scoop up drinking water when out deep on the lakes. The lid prevents spilling no matter how rough the waves.

Lather Shaving Cream (old fashioned soap kind) — The foam or brushless type doesn't work well. All cooking pots should be thoroughly coated before use or you'll have a terrible time cleaning the black off afterward.

It probably goes without saying that suntan cream and sunglasses are a must for most people in the lake country. I mention them so you'll be sure to add them to your list. One other suggestion—if you take air mattresses, include a small bellows-type pump. The time and lung power saved are well worth it.

CANOEING THE BOUNDARY WATERS

FOOD LIST

First Night Meal — Dick and I always packed a small steak, buns, fresh solid tomatoes, onions or other perishable food as a trip starter. Even if the temperature soared into the high 80s, the meat kept cold, sometimes even still a bit frozen. Start out with it solidly frozen and wrap it well in newspapers or other insulating material.

Fresh Eggs — We took six to eight on every trip and never had one break. The trick is to pack them carefully in a round oatmeal box with the oatmeal keeping them well-separated. This way you can carry two kinds of breakfasts safely in one container.

Oleomargarine — You can buy rectangular plastic containers wherever plastic ware is sold that are about right for carrying four sticks. Mold them a little to fit but leave them wrapped. You can pull them out one at a time, and it's less messy and easy to handle.

Bread — We usually enjoyed fresh bread throughout the trip by buying a bakeshop variety in small loaf size in clear plastic bags. On trips of a week or more we took two or three loaves and they stayed fresh and tasty by exposing them to the sun a half hour or more a few times during the trip. Be sure to keep them inside their twister-closed bags. To prevent them from getting squashed in transit we put the loaves (at least two of them) in a small cardboard box inside the food basket. (We found one exactly the right size and kept it through the years.)

Toast — The only successful way we ever worked this out was by buttering the slices of bread lightly on both sides and putting them over the fire in a frying pan. By cutting on the diagonal, two slices can be fit into a large pan with two eggs so they cook at the same time.

Crackers — A luxury we usually included, keeping them in a tall, square plastic container with tight-fitting lid. As they were used it became a handy container for soup and cocoa packets and other small items that are always getting lost in the bottom of the food box or basket.

Peanut Butter and Jam — We carried ours in the Gerry tubes, commonly used by backpackers, which take up little space and eliminate mess—unless the plastic slide tube fastening the bottom comes off! After one such experience we successfully prevented future disasters by inserting toothpicks (round ones) tightly into the folds in the tubes at both ends.

Dried Fruit — Raisins, prunes, apricots and apples were

150

our favorites, cooked into a compote or munched as is. A bag of dried apple slices simmered in a pot with water, sugar and a dash of lemon juice, then sprinkled with cinnamon, makes a satisfying dessert. They're handy for tarts, pies, and coffee cakes too, if you're not camping during berry season.

Flavorings — Though these aren't usually bothered with, we think them important. Lemon juice, ketchup, chili sauce, or whatever you prefer to liven up food, can be taken along in little plastic jars. For really small jars I use plastic pill bottles with screw tops. Small cans of cinnamon or other spices slip easily into corners and crevices without adding much weight. Wilson's bacon bar (or other concentrated meat bars) we found well worth the cost for adding protein and flavor.

Hallmark Beans — (If you can find these—we haven't seen them for a while.) They are precooked pea beans and cook up quickly. Bring along your own brown sugar, mustard and a little dark molasses.

Freeze-dried Dinners — There are many varieties that are well-known and used by many campers. You'll find a good supply of these as well as all sorts of other freeze dried foods at most outfitters. We planned on one dinner a day, plus an extra for an emergency. Other canoeists take less, planning to use fish for several meals. From our observations, you're wise to take the dinners along anyway. If the fishing's good, you can bring them back or eat extra heartily. If not, you won't go hungry.

Kitchen Department Extras — We suggest one long handled spoon for stirring boiling food in the big pots, a turner or pancake flipper, and a sharp knife in a leather sheath (ours was a slender-bladed filet knife). Sandwich baggies I found useful for carrying sandwiches and other lunch items as well as storing leftovers or sticky things in the food box. Aluminum containers with snug fitting lids come in different sizes and can be purchased from most camping goods stores or catalogues. We found our 4x8-inch size just right for keeping a lunch with two sandwiches, dried fruit, nuts and candy bars uncrushed while travelling. It also had many other uses, including a baking pan and mixing "bowl."

A cardboard box that fits into your pack is a good container for your food, or a pack basket that has its own carrying straps and a canvas cover. We ordered ours in medium size from L.L. Bean in Maine. Even when full, its contours fit my back so well that I found it easier to carry than a heavy pack. Dick disagrees, preferring a pack. As in many things, it's a matter of personal choice.

It's plain to see we ate well on our canoe trips. If the

emphasis of your trip is covering distance and includes long portages you would, of course, want to cut frills and lighten your load.

CLOTHING LIST

What kind of clothes you take is again a matter of personal choice, but our essentials included (per person):

1 wool shirt
1 quilted (insulated underwear) jacket
1 nylon windbreaker jacket
1 swimsuit
raingear (hooded jacket and pants)
1 pair jeans or long pants (two in cold weather)
2 pairs shorts (one in cold weather)
3 changes of underwear, socks and lightweight shirts
optional—old, soft moccasins for wear on campsites

I'm mentioning shoes separately because there's such a wide range of preference in the choice of footgear. Many insist on leather hiking boots. We always wore sneakers, thin-soled ones that lace so snugly they move with your foot. We usually carried an extra pair, which enabled us to keep one pair dry, usually.

Plastic carrying bags, the handiest size about 11x15-inch, are nice for clothes and keeping things organized in your pack. One more extra I'd recommend is an old, thin pillowcase (or two) carried flat in the pack and stuffed with enough clothes to make a comfortable pillow at night.

NAVIGATION *

The BWCA is a vast wilderness of lakes, woods and portages—we found many confused people. If you're not sure how to get where you want to go, the first thing to do is "orient" the map. With the help of the compass, sun, shoreline, or other recognizable features of the landscape, position the map on the floor of the canoe so that north on the map corresponds with true north. Next visualize on the map the course you want to take. Look across the lake in the direction you want to go and see if you can find a recognizable landmark, such as an extra tall tree, a rock or a cliff as close as possible to straight ahead. If you can't find a landmark, return to the map and compass and make careful note of the compass bearing (direction) of your course. Now all you need to do is keep the canoe pointed in the right direction, then reorient the map and keep paddling until you get there.

If there is a cross wind, it can blow you off course so it

*This section and those following are mostly written by Dick.

is especially important to use landmarks.

Should an occasion ever arise when you think you're lost (you won't get really lost unless you panic), orient your map with the compass, sun, or stars. Locate on the map points on the shorelines of lakes you might be on which have the same bearing as something close by. Compare shoreline features, islands, and the skyline with what's on the map. Chances are good you'll recognize your location. If you don't, go back to the map and look for an island, an inlet, or something you might find if you moved in one direction or another. With this approach you can work out a plan to locate yourself with a minimum of wasted effort.

PADDLING

If you've never paddled before, the best idea is to take a few lessons at home first. If this isn't possible, get a copy of Calvin Rustrum's "North American Canoe Country" (Macmillan) and read the chapter, The Canoeist's Art. Also, don't be afraid to ask somebody who knows, an outfitter, for example, for a few pointers. Most important, ask about the "J" stroke, the steering stroke used by the stern paddler. Don't waste time and energy steering only by dipping your paddle from one side to the other—only greenhorns do this.

Above all, be cautious about large lakes until you've had experience. Tragedies have resulted from starting out in moderate seas and underestimating the growing size of the waves as you get out beyond the protection of the shore.

CANOES, PORTAGING, ETC

Most of the canoes we saw in the BWCA were aluminum. We used 18-foot Grummans. A canoe is a very seaworthy craft—if it is not overloaded. Often we've seen three adults and their gear in a 17 footer (even a 15 footer!). Usually they make it, but it doesn't take very large waves to swamp them.

Yokes for portaging are available to fit most canoes. However, the pads are small and hard enough to dig into one's shoulders in a short time—especially when the canoe is bounced by a carrier walking a rough trail. I made a yoke of plywood, padded with foam, and covered with Turkish toweling, fitted to my shoulders. With this yoke I find portaging an 85-pound canoe easier than carrying a 45-pound pack.

On a portage your packs and the way they are packed can make a lot of difference. We think "Duluth packs" from the Duluth Tent and Awning Company are best. If you're renting, most outfitters supply these. They are soft packs with straps of broad webbing which distribute the load comfortably on the shoulders. From the viewpoint of comfort while hiking, they're inferior to the packs with frames favored by backpackers but they're easier to stow in a canoe.

When we first bought our own outfit, we ordered so-called "Duluth packs" from a cut-rate mail order house. They were poor quality and wore out fast. If you buy your own, make sure they are made by the Duluth Tent and Awning Company.

The way you pack a pack is important. In each pack containing hard and lumpy things, like cooking kit, flashlight or hatchet, put something large and soft like a tent or air mattresses to cushion your back. The straps of each pack should be adjusted to the right length to make it ride snugly against your back. Larger sized packs come with tump lines (straps to go across your forehead), which some people prefer.

Our first outfit was mostly purchased secondhand from an outfitter. It served very well. The tent was a "four man" nylon about 8-foot square, and high enough to stand in. We found the inside space well worth the carrying weight to have plenty of room for ourselves and the packs when it rained.

On our first trip we rented everything from an outfitter, writing ahead so it would be ready when we arrived. He will supply all your meals, if you prefer, or you can bring some of your own food and pick up other items at his store, as we did. We especially appreciated his friendly interest in helping us plan a canoe route to suit our time and abilities. If you're greenhorns, as we were, we can't think of a better way to get started. Good luck!

OUTFITTERS

Ely area. (Address for all: Ely, Minnesota 55731)
Rom's Canoe Country Outfitters
Canadian Waters Inc.
Border Lakes Outfitters
Boundary Waters Canoe Outfitters
Canadian Border Outfitters
Fall Lake Outfitters
Graystone Outfitters
Moose Lake Wilderness Canoe Trips
Pipestone Outfitting Co.
Quetico-Superior Outfitters
Wilderness Outfitters

Tofte area. (Address: Tofte, Minnesota 55615)
Sawbill Canoe Outfitters

Grand Marais area. (Address for all: Grand Marais, Minnesota 55604)
Nor'Wester Lodge and Canoe Outfitters
Gunflint Northwoods Outfitters
Janet's Seagull Outfitters
Bear Track Outfitting Co.
Bearskin Canoe Outfitters
Chick-Wauk Canoe Outfitters
Jocko's Clearwater Canoe Outfitters
Northpoint Outfitters
Portage Canoe Outfitters
Saganaga Outfitters
Tip of the Trail Outfitters
Tuscarora Canoe Outfitters
Way of the Wilderness Outfitters
Wilderness Waters, Inc.